MW01029413

The B
Psychotherapy

Theories of Psychotherapy Series

Theories of Psychotherapy Series
Jon Carlson and Matt Englar-Carlson, Series Editors

The Basics of Psychotherapy

An Introduction to Theory and Practice

Bruce E. Wampold

American Psychological Association

Washington, DC

Second Printing, December 2010

Published by
American Psychological Association
750 First Street, NE
Washington, DC 20002
www.apa.org

To order
APA Order Department
P.O. Box 92984
Washington, DC 20090-2984
Tel: (800) 374-2721; Direct: (202) 336-5510
Fax: (202) 336-5502; TDD/TTY: (202) 336-6123
Online: www.apa.org/books/
E-mail: order@apa.org

In the U.K., Europe, Africa, and the Middle East, copies may be ordered from
American Psychological Association
3 Henrietta Street
Covent Garden, London
WC2E 8LU England

Typeset in Minion by Circle Graphics, Inc., Columbia, MD

Printer: Edwards Brothers, Ann Arbor, MI
Cover Designer: Minker Design, Sarasota, FL

Cover art: *Lily Rising*, 2005 oil and mixed media on panel in craquelure frame, by Betsy Bauer.

The opinions and statements published are the responsibility of the authors, and such opinions and statements do not necessarily represent the policies of the American Psychological Association.

Library of Congress Cataloging-in-Publication Data

Wampold, Bruce E., 1948-
  The basics of psychotherapy : an introduction to theory and practice / Bruce E. Wampold. — 1st ed.
      p. ; cm.
  Includes bibliographical references and index.
  ISBN-13: 978-1-4338-0750-3
  ISBN-10: 1-4338-0750-5
  1. Psychotherapy—History. I. Title.
  [DNLM: 1. Psychotherapy—methods. 2. Models, Psychological. 3. Psychological Theory. 4. Psychotherapy—history. WM 420 W243b 2010]
  RC480.5.W2764 2010
  616.89'14—dc22

                                                                          2009040974

British Library Cataloguing-in-Publication Data
A CIP record is available from the British Library.

Printed in the United States of America
First Edition

To those who have been in my life and have coconstructed this beautiful life, thank you. Most importantly, to Anna, who has to tolerate me most intimately and loves me all the more.

Contents

Series Preface

Some might argue that in the contemporary clinical practice of psychotherapy, evidence-based intervention and effective outcome have overshadowed theory in importance. Maybe. But, as the editors of this series, we don't propose to take up that controversy here. We do know that psychotherapists adopt and practice according to one theory or another because their experience, and decades of good evidence, suggests that having a sound theory of psychotherapy leads to greater therapeutic success. Still, the role of theory in the helping process can be hard to explain. This narrative about solving problems helps convey theory's importance:

> Aesop tells the fable of the sun and wind having a contest to decide who was the most powerful. From above the earth, they spotted a man walking down the street, and the wind said that he bet he could get his coat off. The sun agreed to the contest. The wind blew and the man held on tightly to his coat. The more the wind blew, the tighter he held. The sun said it was his turn. He put all of his energy into creating warm sunshine and soon the man took off his coat.

What does a competition between the sun and the wind to remove a man's coat have to do with theories of psychotherapy? We think this deceptively simple story highlights the importance of theory as the precursor to any effective intervention—and hence to a favorable outcome. Without a guiding theory, we might treat the symptom without understanding the role of the individual. Or we might create power conflicts with our clients and not understand that, at times, indirect means of helping (sunshine) are often as effective—if not more so—than direct ones (wind). In the absence of theory, we might lose track of the treatment rationale and instead get caught up in, for example, social correctness and not wanting to do something that looks too simple.

What exactly *is* theory? The *APA Dictionary of Psychology* defines theory as "a principle or body of interrelated principles that purports to explain or predict a number of interrelated phenomena." In psychotherapy, a theory is a set of principles used to explain human thought and behavior, including what causes people to change. In practice, a theory creates the goals of therapy and specifies how to pursue them. Haley (1997) noted that a theory of psychotherapy ought to be simple enough for the average therapist to understand, but comprehensive enough to account for a wide range of eventualities. Furthermore, a theory guides action toward successful outcomes while generating hope in both the therapist and client that recovery is possible.

Theory is the compass that allows psychotherapists to navigate the vast territory of clinical practice. In the same ways that navigational tools have been modified to adapt to advances in thinking and ever-expanding territories to explore, theories of psychotherapy have changed over time. The different schools of theories are commonly referred to as waves, the first wave being psychodynamic theories (i.e., Adlerian, psychoanalytic), the second wave learning theories (i.e., behavioral, cognitive–behavioral), the third wave humanistic theories (person-centered, gestalt, existential), the fourth wave feminist and multicultural theories, and the fifth wave postmodern and constructivist theories. In many ways, these waves represent how psychotherapy has adapted and responded to changes in psychology, society, and epistemology as well as to changes in the nature of psychotherapy itself. Psychotherapy and the theories that guide it are dynamic and responsive. The wide variety of theories is also testament to the different ways in which the same human behavior can be conceptualized (Frew & Spiegler, 2008).

It is with these two concepts in mind—the central importance of theory and the natural evolution of theoretical thinking—that we developed the APA Theories of Psychotherapy Series. Both of us are thoroughly fascinated by theory and the range of complex ideas that drive each model. As university faculty members who teach courses on the theories of psychotherapy, we wanted to create learning materials that not only highlight the essence of the major theories for professionals and professionals in training but also clearly bring the reader up to date on the current status of the models. Often in books on theory, the biography of the original theorist overshadows the evolution of the model. In contrast, our intent is to highlight the contemporary uses of the theories as well as their history and context.

As this project began, we faced two immediate decisions: which theories to address and who best to present them. We looked at graduate-level theories of psychotherapy courses to see which theories are being taught, and we explored popular scholarly books, articles, and conferences to determine which theories draw the most interest. We then developed a dream list of authors from among the best minds in contemporary theoretical practice. Each author is one of the leading proponents of that approach as well as a knowledgeable practitioner. We asked each author to review the core constructs of the theory, bring the theory into the modern sphere of clinical practice by looking at it through a context of evidence-based practice, and clearly illustrate how the theory looks in action.

There are 24 titles planned for the series. Each title can stand alone or can be put together with a few other titles to create materials for a course in psychotherapy theories. This option allows instructors to create a course featuring the approaches they believe are the most salient today. To support this end, APA Books has also developed a DVD for each of the approaches that demonstrates the theory in practice with a real client. Some of the DVDs show therapy over six sessions. Contact APA Books for a complete list of available DVD programs (http://www.apa.org/videos).

Throughout the history of psychotherapy, there have been spirited debates about what exactly psychotherapy actually *is*. Other questions have focused on whether psychotherapy actually works and if so, why? Like any form of healing practice, the field of psychotherapy was created in a social context that has influenced the parameters of what psychotherapy (and its various theories of practice) is and what it is not. Before delving into the various forms of psychotherapy, one would be prudent to develop a foundational understanding of their history and an appreciation for the role of theory in that history and in actual practice. *The Basics of Psychotherapy: An Introduction to Theory and Practice* is the opening book in this series, and as such forms its cornerstone. As one of the preeminent contemporary psychotherapy researchers and critics, Dr. Bruce E. Wampold takes a wide view of the history of psychotherapy theory and locates the field's philosophical underpinnings and assumptions. He also defines psychotherapy as a unique form of healing practice and examines how the field has advanced as applied psychological science and how research has evolved and the clientele treated has diversified.

It is our hope that this book will give readers the tools to understand the vast array of theories in current use. By understanding the foundation of psychotherapy provided by Dr. Wampold, the reader can gain the perspective to compare and contrast the many valuable theoretical approaches available. This book can be combined with the other titles in the series to form a complete textbook for a course in psychotherapy theory.

—Jon Carlson and Matt Englar-Carlson

REFERENCES

Frew , J., & Spiegler, M. (2008). *Contemporary psychotherapies for a diverse world.* Boston, MA: Lahaska Press.

Haley, J. (1997). *Leaving home: The therapy of disturbed young people.* New York, NY: Routledge.

Acknowledgments

Rarely, if ever, is a volume truly authored solely by an individual. In our field, an author's knowledge and expertise in psychotherapy accumulate from the intricate and elaborate interaction with colleagues, students, patients, and to a large extent life. Any particular wisdom I have about this subject could not have been attained alone, to be sure.

Much of my thinking about the nature of psychotherapy has come from teaching and working with students. In that regard, my conversations with Dr. Zac Imel over the years have been illuminating—it is a rare student who has the temerity to challenge my thinking to deepen his or her understanding. Zac's intellectual curiosity has pushed me to understand psychotherapy at a deeper level as well, and our collaboration on several projects has realizations that are infused in this book.

Integrating science and practice is not simply an idealized goal, offered to students, knowing that it is rarely possible to achieve. The integration is absolutely necessary if psychotherapy is to progress in a manner that will demonstrably improve the quality of mental health services. My thinking about practice issues and the integration of science and practice has been enhanced through my association with Dr. Teresa Bear, master clinician and trusted colleague. Chapter 3, to a large extent, is a product of these conversations, our work with trainees, and collaborative writing.

What began as an opportunity and turned into a passion would not have been possible without the invitation to write this book by Jon Carlson and Matt Englar-Carlson, the series editors. Their confidence that I could allow my visceral allegiance to psychotherapy as a healing practice to show through my training and role as a scientist is very much appreciated. The unenviable task of subtly reminding me of deadlines, conveying editorial comments, and guiding this process fell to Ed Meidenbauer, whose gentle but firm communications were not always welcome but were always critically valuable. The extraordinary editorial feedback of Jon, Matt, Ed, and reviewers guided the project to what is, I hope and trust, a valuable resource for psychotherapists.

The Basics of
Psychotherapy

1

Introduction

Your new client arrives, 10 minutes late, and sits across from you, uncommunicative. You know from the intake form that the client is a 32-year-old African American man, recently unemployed from a white collar position in the financial industry. He has indicated that he is seeking psychotherapy because his wife has informed him that she and their children will leave him if he does not reduce his alcohol consumption and abusive language. He is well dressed and groomed, but his affect is flat, he appears fatigued, and his eyes are bloodshot.

Many thoughts and even more questions are running through your mind. Is he depressed? Is his alcohol use related to his recent loss of employment, or does he have a history of substance use? Are his red eyes due to alcohol use, crying, or some medical condition? Unemployment can elicit feelings of self-doubt and negative attributions about self, but are his problems simply related to change in his job status? Or was he terminated because of poor performance due to his mental condition? What contextual issues are relevant—race, culture, society, employment, or any other issue? Is the marital problem a result of the unemployment or a cause of many other issues in the client's life? Or perhaps there is a history of depression that has been exacerbated by the change in employment status. What does he want from therapy—is he ready to make changes, or is he there because of the ultimatum from his wife? Are there other issues yet to be uncovered? But the most urgent question is, What do I say to him, at this moment, and how do I say it? And how do I respond to his reaction to my comments?

This very brief vignette poignantly illustrates how complex the task of therapy can be and typically is. There is much important background knowledge needed—a firm understanding of biological, social, ecological, cultural, and cognitive bases of behavior. But what is most important in psychotherapy is a good road map of how therapy unfolds—a guide to action. A map is a representation of reality, and one would not set out across the country without one. In psychotherapy, the representation of reality used to guide therapy is theory. Theory provides the framework for therapeutic action—which questions to ask, what to attend to, how to respond to client verbal and nonverbal behavior, when and how to intervene, and how to assess progress. Every aspect of therapy is saturated with the theoretical perspective of the therapist. As will become apparent, there is no one "best" road map for therapy; rather, there are a plethora of viable theories from which to choose.

This series is devoted to introducing you to psychotherapy theories. This is a dynamic process, in an important way. You meet the theories, but they do not represent simply information to be learned. The goal is not to be a well-versed and conversant theorist—the goal is to use theory to be an effective therapist. In the process of becoming a therapist, you will need to master a few of these theories as your road map. Some of the theories will feel more comfortable and logical to you than others. Similarly, some theories will be more compatible with the client than others. So it is not simply a case of which theory is best for you—the most important issue is that the choice of theory ultimately is about what is most effective with this client, as *used* by you. Again, the process is dynamic and complex.

A short introduction to psychotherapy as a healing practice is presented in this chapter. Subsequent chapters examine the history of psychotherapy, the role of theory in psychotherapy, and, finally, the research about how psychotherapy works.

PSYCHOTHERAPY AS A HEALING PRACTICE

Psychotherapy is widely accepted as a legitimate and beneficial healing practice in the United States and in many other countries. It is estimated that more than 10 million Americans receive psychotherapy annually (Olfson et al., 2002; Wang et al., 2005). Of those who avail themselves of services for psychological distress in the United States, about 40% receive psychotherapy from a psychologist, social worker, or counselor; the remainder receive services from a psychiatrist (13%), general practice physician (9%), human services professional (religious or spiritual advisor or counselor not in a mental health setting; 9%), or complementary or alternative medicine provider or group (e.g., chiropractor, self-help group; 32%; Druss et al., 2007). It is estimated that between $5.7 and $9.6 billion is spent on psychotherapy in the United States annually (Langreth, 2007; Minami & Wampold, 2008; Olfson et al., 2002). Clearly, psychotherapy is an established practice and a major industry. However, the status of psychotherapy as a healing practice is complex.

The first question that should be asked is whether or not psychotherapy works. The answer, which is explored in more detail in chapter 4 of this volume, is a resounding yes. The benefits of psychotherapy are clear—those receiving psychotherapy achieve much better outcomes that they would have had they not received psychotherapy (Lambert & Ogles, 2004; Wampold, 2001b, 2007). Indeed, psychotherapy is more effective than many accepted, but expensive, medical practices and has no aversive side effects. In clinical trials, psychotherapy has been shown to be effective for the treatment of depression, anxiety, marital dissatisfaction, substance abuse, health problems (e.g., smoking, pain, eating disorders), and sexual dysfunction and with various populations, including children, adolescents, adults, and elders (Chambless et al., 1998). Psychotherapy stacks up well against medications for various mental disorders, most notably depression and anxiety disorders, and is more enduring (i.e., less prone to relapse) and less resistant to additional courses of treatment (Hollon, Stewart, & Strunk, 2006; Imel, McKay, Malterer, & Wampold, 2008; Leykin et al., 2007). It has been found that psychotherapy, as practiced in the real world, is as effective as psychotherapy delivered in the controlled conditions of randomized clinical trials (Minami & Wampold, 2008; see chap. 4, this volume).

Despite the acceptance and effectiveness of psychotherapy, there are some concerns to note. First and foremost, most people who need mental health services do not receive care of any kind. A recent national survey in the United States found that fewer than 40% of people who would be classified as having a mental disorder (e.g., a disorder listed in the *Diagnostic and Statistical Manual of Mental Disorders [DSM]*; American Psychiatric Association, 2000) received mental health treatment (Druss et al., 2007). The conclusion drawn from such national surveys is that "most people with mental disorders in the United States remain either untreated or poorly treated" (Wang et al., 2005, p. 629). Moreover, this problem is worse for clients most in need: "Unmet need for treatment is greatest in traditionally underserved groups, including elderly persons, racial–ethnic minorities, those with low incomes, those without insurance, and residents of rural areas" (Wang et al., 2005, p. 629). The problem, it seems, is not that psychotherapy is not effective, but rather that this practice is not being delivered to people who need it (see chap. 4, this volume).

It is not entirely clear why more people do not use psychotherapy. One important reason is that increasingly medications are used to treat mental disorders. Between $5.7 billion and $9.6 billion is spent annually on psychotherapy in the United States—in contrast, the annual sales of antidepressants alone in the United States is over $13 billion (Langreth, 2007)! A clear trend over the course of several national surveys is that the use of medical services for mental disorders, which presumably involves psychotropic medication, has increased over time. From the early 1990s to the early 2000s, there has been an increase in the use of psychiatrists, general medical combined with mental health specialists (i.e., psychotherapy), and general medicine to treat psychological problems (Wang et al., 2006).

On the other hand, it appears that the use of psychotherapy has declined during that period (Minami & Wampold, 2008). There are many factors that might account for these trends, including advertising by pharmaceutical companies, reimbursement benefits of health insurance and government, the hubris of the medical system, and so forth. A Harris Poll conducted in conjunction with *Psychology Today* and PacifiCare Behavioral Health (Harris Interactive, 2004) was undertaken in 2004 to determine why people use or don't use psychotherapy. Prominent in the list of reasons is the cost: Many reported that psychotherapy is too expensive (39%) or that their insurance coverage for psychotherapy was not adequate (26%). Disturbingly, given the evidence for the effectiveness of psychotherapy, the belief that psychotherapy would not be helpful was a reason given by many (32%). Of course, many simply thought that their problems were not serious enough to warrant treatment (35%). Surprising to many was that fact that stigma associated with therapy was less often cited as a reason not to seek psychotherapy than was expense, beliefs about effectiveness, and severity, although more than a fifth of respondents (22%) did indicate that stigma was a problem. More than half of the respondents indicated that mental health services were difficult to obtain. So despite the established effectiveness of psychotherapy and its widespread use, there remain many individuals, particularly from traditionally underserved populations, who would benefit from psychotherapy but do not use it.

There is a perception that psychotherapy is being provided to clients who really are not distressed—that is, that psychotherapy is being delivered to the "worried well." Interestingly, of those receiving mental health services, about 40% had experienced the symptoms of a *DSM* diagnosis in the prior 12 months, 18% had experienced the symptoms of a *DSM* diagnosis in their lifetimes, and 13% had or had previously had other indicators of need, such as subclinical symptoms or a stressful life event. Fewer than 4% of those receiving mental health services had no indicator of need. Of those 4%, only 16% were receiving psychotherapy services from a nonpsychiatrist. So only about 0.5% to 1.0% of the general population were receiving psychotherapy with no indicator of need, according to the survey criteria (Druss et al., 2007).

One should keep in mind that psychotherapy is a relatively new practice. It was about a century and a half ago that Freud developed the "talking cure," so the use of psychotherapy is just emerging as a legitimate treatment in the United States and around the world relative to the practice of medicine, which has existed since ancient times (Pritz, 2002). As is

discussed in chapter 2 of this volume, psychotherapy is an evolving, culturally embedded practice (see, e.g., Fancher, 1995; Pritz, 2002). The profession, for better or worse, has evolved from long-term intensive treatments
(two or three times a week for several years) to, for the most part, focused
and brief interventions (Engel, 2008). However, the field continues to
emerge and change. Science produces new evidence, policies change, payment mechanisms evolve, and people influence the profession. Only one
thing is safe to say: Psychotherapy will change to meet the times.

PSYCHOTHERAPY DEFINED

To this point, psychotherapy has been referenced without a proper definition. So before continuing, psychotherapy is defined and issues related
to that definition are discussed. What will be clear is that the boundaries
of what is considered psychotherapy are fuzzy.

Psychotherapy belongs to a class of healing practices that involve
"talk" as the medium to address psychological distress. In many ways, psychotherapy is an amorphous practice, as it is delivered by a variety of professionals and paraprofessionals, including psychologists, psychiatrists,
counselors, marriage and family therapists, and social workers; uses a variety of techniques based on a variety of theoretical models; and is closely
allied with a number of related professions and practices, such as personal
coaching, support groups, vocational counseling, guidance programs, and
self-help programs (Engel, 2008). The focus of this series is on what might
be termed theories of "mainstream" psychotherapy, although issues related
to practices on the margins are discussed at important junctures.

Keeping in mind that no definition of *psychotherapy* will be entirely
adequate, the following definition is offered to define the practice:

> Psychotherapy is a primarily interpersonal treatment, based on psy-
> chological principles, and involves a trained therapist and a client
> who has a mental disorder, problem, or complaint, is intended by the
> therapist to be remedial for the client disorder, problem, or com-
> plaint, and is adapted or individualized for the particular client and
> his or her disorder, problem, or complaint. (Wampold, 2001b, p. 3)

Examining aspects of this definition will help clarify the boundaries of psychotherapy vis-à-vis other similar practices, but keep in mind that there are aspects of the definitions, boundaries, and practices about which many would quibble. Yet as various theories are discussed, it is important to confine the practice of psychotherapy.

First, psychotherapy is primarily an interpersonal intervention and as such has been characterized often in its history as *talk therapy.* That is, psychotherapy involves an interpersonal relationship between therapist and client, and the conversation between the therapist and the client *is* psychotherapy, in many respects. Of course, the client may enact many behaviors within the therapy session or outside of the session that are generally accepted as therapeutic, such as an exercise involving exposure in which the client approaches some feared situation (e.g., a person with social phobia is instructed to talk to a potential romantic partner). Nevertheless, the means of delivering the important aspects of psychotherapy is the verbal interaction (Wampold, 2007). It is unclear whether some modern practices, such as technology-assisted interventions, should be classified as psychotherapy. Telephone counseling or video-based interventions clearly involve an interpersonal relationship, although not face-to-face. Many would classify an Internet interaction in chat mode as interpersonal and language mediated and thus could be classified as psychotherapy, particularly to members of a generation in which many important interpersonal relationships transpire electronically.

The interpersonal relationship criterion, however, importantly removes various environmental interventions, such as those based on classical conditioning (e.g., token reinforcement programs in the schools), which may effectively change behavior but which are not psychotherapy, in the sense used in this series. Indeed, any psychological intervention that does not depend primarily on language as the mode of delivery is not psychotherapy as defined here. Thus, clients without cognitive abilities to communicate linguistically (e.g., infants, individuals with severe communication disorders) cannot in this sense participate in psychotherapy. Of course, this does not preclude other psychological interventions.

Healing practices generally are embedded in a belief system (Wampold, 2007); the belief system of psychotherapy is generically psychological. That is, the underlying rationale for any psychotherapeutic treatment must be psychological. As will be apparent in this series, there are very many different psychological theories that can be usefully applied to develop various psychotherapies. Again, there are interventions that are on the margins, including, for example, the "body therapies." The rationale for massage therapy is more physiological than psychological, although other body approaches, including, for example, Reichian therapies, have purported psychological bases, albeit controversial ones. In this series, the discussion is restricted to psychotherapies that have cogent psychological bases.

Another commonality of healing practices is that the healer has special characteristics that separate him or her from laypeople and an authority based on status and knowledge (Boyer, 2001; Frank & Frank, 1991; Wampold, 2007). Accordingly, psychotherapy in this series is restricted to those practices that involve a trained therapist, although it is recognized that although most psychotherapy is practiced by degreed and credentialed therapists, occasionally psychotherapy is conducted by paraprofessionals or others without degrees and credentials but with specialized training (e.g., graduate student therapists, some substance abuse counselors). However, psychotherapy is differentiated from any practices conducted informally (e.g., between friends), as an unofficial part of duties (e.g., hairdressers, bartenders), or not generally sanctioned as professional services (e.g., services provided by a religious figure not otherwise trained and recognized as a therapist). This definition thus excludes indigenous healing practices, although there is a close relationship between such practices and psychotherapy (Wampold, 2007).

Notice that the definition used here refers to a client *disorder, problem,* or *complaint.* Intentionally, the definition does not necessarily characterize the distress as a *mental disorder,* as many psychotherapies eschew such classifications as unhelpful and even stigmatizing. Nevertheless, psychotherapy is a practice that addresses some felt distress and in this regard does not include interventions that are primarily preventive, such as drug prevention programs. This discussion raises a critical issue about whether interventions with individuals who have not presented voluntarily can be classified as psychotherapy. In some contexts, clients are mandated to seek treatment (e.g., by the criminal justice system), are pressured by family members, or are referred by schools; such clients are reluctant participants and often do not engage in therapy in a manner that characterizes psychotherapy (Wampold, 2007). Nevertheless, clients vary in their motivation and readiness for change, and of course it is the responsibility of the therapist to engage the client and increase the desire for change (Moyers, Miller, & Hendrickson, 2005; Prochaska & Norcross, 2002). However, as will be seen, psychotherapy depends centrally on the notion of a collaborative relationship in which therapist and client have agreements about the tasks and goals of therapy.

The definition of psychotherapy importantly stipulates that the treatment delivered is intended by the therapist to be therapeutic. Clients in any healing practice expect that the healer believes in the effectiveness of the practice, and psychotherapy clients are no different. Indeed, research supports the claim that therapist allegiance to the treatment is associated with psychotherapy outcomes (Wampold, 2001b). Typically, therapists in practice have allegiance to the treatment delivered, but occasionally treatment protocols are mandated for various reasons, resulting in therapists delivering a treatment that they do not believe is optimally therapeutic. Although one could classify the delivery of a protocol by a doubting therapist as psychotherapy, the discussion here pertains to treatments faithfully delivered. Moreover, treatments delivered in clinical trials by therapists who are aware that the treatment is not intended to be therapeutic (e.g., supportive counseling) are considered to be sham treatments—this recognition is critical to understanding the evidence about psychotherapy efficacy derived from clinical trials (see Wampold, 2001b), as discussed further in chapter 4.

A final aspect of the definition of psychotherapy is that it is individualized to the client and his or her concerns. That is, the therapist listens intently to the client and then shapes the therapy to respond to the client, both in terms of client characteristics and the client's concern. There are a number of programs designed to address particular problems and/or to improve lives that do not involve such individualization, such as fixed relaxation protocols, meditation, and movement programs (e.g., dance therapy). Although these types of interventions may be effective, they are not psychotherapy in the sense used in this series.

Psychotherapy is often delivered to more than one client at a time, as is the case in group therapy, couples therapy, and family therapy. These variations are often referred to as *modalities*. Frequently, standard individual protocols, such as cognitive–behavioral treatments, are modified to be delivered in group formats, whereas other times treatments are unique to the modality (e.g., multisystemic family therapy is necessarily a family modality). The definition of psychotherapy should be broad enough to encompass various modalities as well as theoretical perspectives.

As mentioned, *psychotherapy* is a generic term in the sense that the practitioners of psychotherapy belong to a variety of professions, including counseling, social work, medicine, and psychology, among others, and within each profession, there are various specialties that take various perspectives on the training and practice of psychotherapy. For example, in psychology, there are specialties in school, counseling, and clinical psychology. Psychotherapy is practiced in a variety of settings, including private practice, community agencies, hospitals and clinics, and counseling centers (Minami & Wampold, 2008; VandenBos, Cummings, & DeLeon, 1992). Moreover, therapists receive payment from a variety of sources, including the client directly, managed care and other insurance companies, institutions (e.g., universities, as in college counseling centers), various government agencies (e.g., Medicare in the United States, national health services in many countries), and nonprofit agencies.

PURPOSE OF THE BOOK

This book is intended to introduce the emerging professional to psychotherapy. George Santayana (1905) famously noted, "Those who cannot remember the past are condemned to repeat it" (p. 284). The same can be said about psychotherapy—a thorough understanding of how psychotherapy evolved, the forces that were and are brought to bear on it, its place in the healing practices, and the scientific evidence that supports its use are absolutely necessary to train clinicians and researchers to carry the profession forward in the 21st century.

This is the first book in a series on theoretical models of psychotherapy. The backbone of psychotherapy is theory. An atheoretical collection of techniques is not sufficient—every professional and most craftspeople know much about the underlying principles of their domains. Theory is the scaffolding that holds the enterprise together. Research evidence, therapeutic techniques, clinical expertise, skill acquisition, and all the rest become amorphous chaos without this scaffolding.

Theories in psychotherapy have evolved, as is discussed in some depth in chapter 2 of this volume (see Cushman, 1992; Fancher, 1995; Wampold, 2001b). Freud introduced psychoanalysis, and it was the predominant model for decades—but the second and third forces of behavioral therapy and humanistic therapy, respectively, entered the arena in the mid-20th century. A fourth force, multicultural counseling, appeared recently. However, by most accounts there are hundreds of theories, some closely aligned with a central theme and others quite different. Making the landscape more complex is that many practicing therapists consider themselves eclectic or integrative (Norcross, Hedges, & Castle, 2002). How is a graduate student supposed to make sense of a field with so many theories? This series is designed to lend coherence to this diversity.

This introductory book sets the stage in three ways. First, the historical context is described. Chapter 2 addresses the following questions: How did psychotherapy originate and prosper? What are the key developments, and who influenced the field? How did (and does) the cultural context shape the development of psychotherapy as a healing practice?

Chapter 3 discusses the critical question, What role does theory play in the practice of psychotherapy? Theory is absolutely necessary for practice, and theory guides how therapists think about their cases and what they do in psychotherapy. Without theory, there is no psychotherapy. The choice of particular theory involves a calculus involving both the therapist and the patient, as discussed in chapter 3. As well, the philosophy of science bases of various theories are discussed to demonstrate that determining the relative worth of various theories is problematic.

Chapters 4 and 5 review the research evidence. Psychotherapy is a psychology-based endeavor and, as such, rests on an empirical base to the extent possible. Therapists should be knowledgeable about the relevant research and incorporate it as appropriate to ensure that their clients benefit. Although the review in chapters 4 and 5 is relatively brief, the following questions are addressed: Does psychotherapy work? Are some psychotherapies more effective than others? What do we know about the delivery of psychotherapy in the real world? How does psychotherapy work?

Finally, chapter 6 presents a summary and reiterates the importance of theory in practice.

2

Psychotherapy Theory: The Historical Context

Knowledge of the history and cultural context of psychotherapy is critical in understanding current practices, learning how to conduct psychotherapy, and promoting the practice within various professions and within various societal institutions. This chapter examines the origins and development, as well as the current status, of psychotherapy.

A history can trace the antecedents of the present, which provides an important story for those engaged in a profession. As important or more important, however, is an examination of what was omitted from the story (Wampold & Bhati, 2004). The development of psychotherapy as a profession and as the object of research is complex. An appreciation of the history enriches understanding and provides perspectives on science and practice that are otherwise ignored.

Messer (2004) called attention to "psychology's dual heritage" (p. 586), formed from the scientific and the humanistic traditions. The scientific tradition has provided evidence that psychotherapy is remarkably effective and has established the legitimacy of psychotherapy in the health care delivery system. The humanistic tradition has laid the foundation for the caring, empathic, and meaning-making aspects of the practice of psychotherapy. Unfortunately, this dual heritage has often divided the discipline, scientists and practitioners emphasizing different aspects of the same endeavor. On the one hand, the scientists have often found applications of psychology to be not particularly scientific. Those aligned with humanistic aspects of psychotherapy, on the other hand, have perceived scientific investigations to be focused on aspects of psychotherapy that are irrelevant to what they see as the essence of the endeavor (Wampold, 2007). Nevertheless, both scientists and practitioners are committed to the same goal: helping clients overcome their difficulties and lead more fulfilled and meaningful lives. A review of the history gives some insight into the two traditions and is critical to understanding the role of psychotherapeutic theories in the science and practice of psychotherapy.

SOCIAL CONTEXT FOR THE ORIGINS OF PSYCHOTHERAPY

One of the characteristic features of humans is the modification of behavior through social influence (de Waal, 2006). That is, social groups have a strong influence on the thoughts and behavior of individual members. Societies, from the origins of human civilization, have used various healing practices, and central to those practices have been designated healers as well as socially accepted healing rituals (A. K. Shapiro & Shapiro, 1997). For most of human civilization, mental and physical disorders were not distinct, and various mechanisms, none of which were "scientific" in today's sense, were used to explain aberrations from normality.

In Europe in the late 19th century, a convergence of intellectual forces gave rise to *talk therapy* as a means of treating various disorders. The scientific method was becoming accepted as a means to understand the physical and biological world, creating the context for mechanistic explanations for physical phenomena (Newtonian physics) and natural selection mechanisms for biological organisms (Darwinian evolution). This intellectual curiosity was motivation to form a scientific theory of the inner world (i.e., the mind), which could then be applied to the treatment of disorders that had no biological basis (i.e., to mental disorders). From that cauldron emerged Sigmund Freud, among others, who created systems for understanding normal and abnormal mental states and treatment of disorders of the mind (Makari, 2008). Freud was immensely successful in creating a synthesis of extant intellectual and scientific ideas to create what is now called *psychoanalysis.* Psychoanalysis evolved into a grand theory, in that it encompassed all aspects of the conscious and unconscious as well a method to treat all disorders, from the mildly neurotic to the most severely psychotic and everything in between.

Many trace the origins of psychotherapy in the United States to Freud. In 1909, Freud gave his influential lecture at Clark University to a receptive audience. Indeed, William James, the preeminent psychologist during the first decades of the 20th century, is said to have proclaimed, when he met Freud, "Yours is the psychology of the future" (Cushman, 1992). Within a short period of time, psychoanalysis would become the predominant approach to psychotherapy and, as well, would capture the imagination of the American public (Cushman, 1992; Makari, 2008).

Interestingly, talk therapy existed in the United States in the decades prior to Freud's lecture. Toward the end of the 19th century, an increasing number of Americans were involved with *mind cures,* the most popular of which were Christian Science and the New Thought movement, two practices that attempted to use the mind to cure illness and improve the quality of life. Retrospectively, these movements may seem to be anarchistic or marginalized religious practices, but they were immensely popular during this period (Caplan, 1998; Harrington, 2008; Taylor, 1999).

The popularity of practices that claimed to physically heal through mind, faith, or spirituality created significant issues for medicine. During this period, medicine itself was just emerging as a scientifically based profession. One of the cornerstones of modern scientific medicine is *materialism,* a philosophical term that stipulates that matter is the sole basis of reality. Thus, in the early 20th century, medicine was increasingly adamant that any bodily state, including most importantly illness, had a physical cause and that any treatment cured by altering the biological system (Caplan, 1998; Harrington, 2008). Medicine was eager to scientifically demonstrate that those who reported purported cures based on unscientific principles were charlatans. Indeed, the discrediting of Franz Anton Mesmer's cures, which were based on theories of animal magnetism, has been heralded as a crown jewel of the scientific method (Gould, 1989; Wampold, 2001a; Wampold & Bhati, 2004).

As opposed to Europe, where Freud's psychoanalysis arguably was accepted in the medical community (at the time, most practitioners were medical doctors), in the United States medicine was particularly resistant to mind cures, a situation that was exacerbated by the fact that many involved in these movements were also enamored with mesmerism and the occult (Caplan, 1998; Cushman, 1992). However, the legitimacy of mind cures increased as the practices became less religious and psychologists and even some physicians became involved. The Boston School of Psychopathology, which was initiated in 1859 and included among its members the psychologists William James and G. Stanley Hall, as well as neurologists and psychiatrists, was demonstrating influence in the professions. In 1906, the Emmanuel movement was founded by physicians and Christian ministers, an attractive collaboration between those interested in the psyche and those interested in the moral aspects of behavior. In this organization, lectures and services were followed by the administration of "therapy" to patients (Caplan, 1998; Taylor, 1999). For medicine, two aspects of the Emmanuel movement were particularly troublesome. First, individuals were being "treated" by psychic methods, which failed to conform to the materialistic stance of modern medicine; no biological etiology for distress was identified; and the intervention did not target any biological process. Second, that the treatments were being delivered by nonphysicians was very threatening from a professional perspective (Caplan, 1998).

Medicine faced a dilemma with the increasing popularity of psychic treatments for mental disorders. Either they could continue to profess disdain for the psychic treatments or they could co-opt the practice as a medical treatment (Caplan, 1998; Mosher & Richards, 2005). The popularity of these talk therapies was threatening, and medicine acted in its own best interest by co-opting the mind cures. Soon, psychotherapy became the province of physicians—to the chagrin of Freud, by the way (Mosher &

Richards, 2005). As is often the case with professions, the action was taken in the name of public safety. The prominent physician John K. Mitchell declared, "Most earnestly should we insist that the *treatment* of a patient, whether it be surgical, medical, or psychic, should for the safety of the public, be in the hands of a doctor" (cited in Caplan, 1998, p. 142).

Before psychic methods could be incorporated into the set of physician treatments, however, the religious and spiritual bases would have to be shed in lieu of a secular and scientific explanation of mental distress and its remediation (Caplan, 1998; Harrington, 2008; Makari, 2008). Freud's psychoanalysis provided the explanation needed by medicine to be able to incorporate psychic treatments into a profession based on materialism. In one sense, Freud brilliantly synthesized various strands to develop a comprehensive theory that was acceptable to the professions and then embraced by the public (Makari, 2008). The merits of Freud's theories can, and have been, debated. However, the unarguable beauty and power of this theory, in the historical context, are compellingly apparent. Freud's development of psychoanalysis and its introduction to the United States illustrated the immense influence that a cogent theory can have on a field.

Freud's psychoanalytic theory fit nicely into a medical model. Although Freud's theoretical propositions evolved over the years (and to a significant degree prior to the lecture at Clark), the general frame was similar: (a) Hysterical symptoms (and later most mental distress, as well as many physical disorders) were caused by the repression of some traumatic event (real or imagined) in the unconscious, (b) the nature of the symptom was related to the event, and (c) the symptom could be relieved by insight into the relationship between the event and the symptom. Insight was fostered through a variety of techniques over Freud's life, including hypnosis, direct questions, dream interpretation, transference interpretation, and free association. An important aspect of medical treatments was that the treatment is specific for the disorder, which is to say that the specific ingredients of the treatment remediate the disorder through the hypothesized mechanism; psychoanalysis was specific in the sense that the *insight* was the critical ingredient. The notion of specificity in psychotherapy continued to be a central issue, as will be discussed later.

Of course, it was tremendously important that Freud was a physician. Later, psychoanalysis would be severely criticized for introducing mentalistic constructs (e.g., the ego and the id), which were unobservable, but in 1909 that seemed unimportant. One could make the case that the beginning of psychotherapy as a medical practice in the United States originated when psychoanalytic theory was accepted by U.S. medicine and when the practice of psychoanalysis was limited to physicians.

There are two critical (and related) aspects of this history of the origins of psychotherapy in the United States. First, in the transition from pre-Freudian practices such as Christian Science, the Emmanuel movement, and the Boston School of Psychopathology to psychoanalysis, the moral, religious, and spiritual elements were sloughed off, and psychotherapy became a professional and thus necessarily a secular activity. Second, psychotherapy, as a practice but not yet a profession, became associated with medicine. Although psychiatry has for the most part abandoned psychotherapy in favor of biological psychiatry, the association of psychotherapy with medicine has continued, in many explicit as well as implicit ways.

THE EMERGENCE OF COMPETING THEORIES

As was clear, Freud's psychoanalytic theory fit nicely into a medical model and provided a cogent theoretical basis that was acceptable to medicine; indeed, it was used to facilitate the emergence of psychotherapy as a medical practice. Clearly, however, psychoanalysis was a fluid theory. For example, the origins of the unconscious material vacillated among such causes as early sexual abuse, fantasized taboo sexual desires, any trauma (e.g., military trauma), anxiety-producing thoughts, and so forth. These and other alterations of psychoanalytic theory were generated by criticism as much as or more than by advances in science (Harrington, 2008; Makari, 2008). Nevertheless, Freud was adamant that cures could not be attained unless his protocols were followed precisely, causing rifts with such luminaries as Joseph Breuer, Alfred Adler, and Carl Jung, who proposed theoretical variations and different therapeutic actions. The bases of these arguments were centered on the nature of pathology and the specificity of treatments;

many of the contentions were about libidinal aspects of pathology and whether cures depended on revealing unconscious sexual conflicts (Makari, 2008). At the time, of course, there was little research that could corroborate or refute Freud's claims.

In the first decades of the 20th century, the positivist movement (see chap. 3 of this volume as well) was emphasizing observation as the foundation of "science" and was eschewing mediating theoretical constructs that could not be observed. Accordingly, one assault on psychoanalytic theory came from those who claimed that clinical applications of psychology should be based on laboratory research and observable behavior and those who avoided mentalistic constructs such as the ego and id. Ivan Petrovich Pavlov's work on classical conditioning detailed how animals acquired a conditioned response, how the conditioned response could be extinguished (i.e., extinction), and how experimental neurosis could be induced. In the famous "Little Albert" study, John B. Watson and Rosalie Rayner demonstrated that a fear response could be conditioned by pairing an unconditioned stimulus of fear (viz., loud noise) with a conditioned stimulus (viz., a rat) so that the conditioned stimulus elicited the fear response (J. B. Watson & Rayner, 1920). Although Watson and Rayner did not attempt to treat Albert's fear, Mary Cover Jones used the classical conditioning paradigm to desensitize another boy's fear of rabbits by gradually decreasing the proximity of the stimulus (i.e., a rabbit).

The first clinical application of learning theory involved the procedure termed *systematic desensitization*, developed by Joseph Wolpe, who like Freud was a medical doctor. Disenchanted with psychoanalysis as a method to treat his patients, he used the work of Pavlov, Watson, Rayner, and Jones to study how eating, an incompatible response to fear, could be used to reduce phobic reactions of cats, which he had previously conditioned. He extended that paradigm by using progressive relaxation, developed by the physiologist Edmund Jacobson, as the incompatible response to treat anxious patients. These clinical applications of classical conditioning were described in Wolpe's seminal book *Psychotherapy by Reciprocal Inhibition*, published in 1958, which interestingly enough was published about the same time as the restriction on the practice of psychoanalysis by physicians was being relaxed.

Behaviorism has been labeled the "second force" in psychotherapy, and it was clear from the beginning that the behaviorists had a certain disdain for the "first force," psychoanalysis, due to the "unscientific" nature of theory and the lack of connection to observable phenomena. As early as 1920, J. B. Watson and Rayner ridiculed the psychoanalytic foundations:

> The Freudians twenty years from now, unless their hypotheses change, when they come to analyze Albert's fear of a seal skin coat—assuming that he comes to analysis at that age—will probably tease from him the recital of a dream which upon their analysis will show that Albert at three years of age attempted to play with the pubic hair of the mother and was scolded violently for it. (p. 14)

Fishman and Franks (1992) described Watson's focus on behaviorism as science:

> According to Watson, if psychology were to become a science—as he defined the word—it must become materialistic (as opposed to mentalistic), mechanistic (as opposed to anthropomorphic), deterministic (as opposed to accepting of free will), and objective (as opposed to subjective). (p. 162)

As cognition gained a more prominent position in experimental psychology, some behaviorists expanded their models to incorporate the client's thoughts. This represented a major change in behaviorism, as cognitions are private events and are not available to an objective observer. Several assumptions underlie cognitive–behavioral therapy (CBT; see Fishman & Franks, 1992): (a) Humans do not simply respond to stimuli in the environment, but rather to a mental representation of the stimuli; (b) much of human learning is cognitively mediated; (c) the client's cognitions (attitudes, expectations, attributions) are central to psychopathology, and changing these cognitions can reduce distress; and (d) the role of the therapist involves assessing maladaptive cognitions and serving as an educator and consultant to the client, designing learning experiences that will change the cognitions and maladaptive behaviors and emotions that are related to the cognitions. The early cognitive theorists and researchers included

Albert Ellis, Aaron Beck, Michael Mahoney, and Donald Meichenbaum, some of whom were behaviorists and some of whom migrated toward the cognitive–behavioral theory from disparate approaches (e.g., Albert Ellis was trained and practiced as a psychoanalyst).

It is unclear whether cognitive therapy is best represented as a subsystem of behavior therapy (Fishman & Franks, 1992) or should be classified as a distinct paradigm (Arnkoff & Glass, 1992). To some, cognitive processes can be tested and assessed in ways that are similar to behaviors, can be changed via behavioral principles, and can be integrated with more traditional behavioral techniques. Others consider some cognitive therapies as distinct from behavior therapy (contrast Arnkoff & Glass, 1992, and Fishman & Franks, 1992). Nevertheless, cognitive and behavioral treatments share many theoretical, conceptual, historical, and political similarities. Arguably, CBT has become the predominant theoretical approach worldwide; to some, psychotherapy is CBT. A report on National Public Radio's *All Things Considered* (Spiegel, 2004) on the treatment of a woman suffering social phobia began by stating, "Cognitive–behavioral therapy is the fastest growing and most rigorously studied form of psychotherapy. It is fast becoming what people in America mean when they say they are getting therapy." Although some would dispute whether CBT is deserving of this prominence, the development and scientific testing of CBT have rendered psychotherapy a cost-effective and respected intervention in health care systems in the United States and in many other countries.

After World War II, a "third force" in psychotherapy, referred to as the *humanistic* and *experiential* approaches, emerged from modernity and attempts to make meaning of life given the ravages of war and the Holocaust (Engel, 2008). Theoretical approaches in this class of treatments are loosely based on the humanistic philosophers (e.g., Kierkegaard, Husserl, and Heidegger) and have in common (a) a phenomenological perspective (i.e., therapy must involve understanding the client's world), (b) an assumption that humans seek growth and actualization, (c) a belief that humans are self-determining, and (d) a respect for every individual, regardless of his or her role or actions (Rice & Greenberg, 1992). The best known of the humanistic therapies are person-centered therapy, developed and explained by Carl Rogers; gestalt therapy, as proposed by Frederick "Fritz" Perls; and existential approaches, exemplified by the work of Rollo May and Victor Frankl. Humanistic approaches were distinctly nonmedical and eschewed for the most part the experimental roots of learning theory, although ironically it was Rogers who first recorded counseling sessions and investigated the process of psychotherapy. In many ways, these approaches are more aligned with philosophy than science and medicine.

Humanistic approaches have developed over the years, in the same way that psychodynamic and behavioral approaches have evolved. Leslie Greenberg, Robert Elliott, and Kirk Schneider, among others, have continued to develop and study the change process in humanistic and experiential therapies (Elliott & Greenberg, 2007; Elliott, Greenberg, & Lietaer, 2004; L. S. Greenberg, Elliott, & Lietaer, 1994; Schneider, 2008). One prominent variant, which has been extensively investigated in terms of both process and outcome, is referred to as *process experiential therapy* or *emotion-focused therapy* and rests on six principles. First, emotional experiencing is central to human functioning and is a dynamic process. Second, the presence and authenticity of the therapist allow the human attachment process to occur such that new client experiences occur. Third, agency and self-determination are seen as an evolved and adaptive human motivation. Fourth, wholeness is adaptive and mediated by emotion; excessive executive control of emotion is unhealthy. Fifth, individual differences (diversity) and pluralism, along with equality and empowerment, are goals to be pursued. Sixth, growth stems from innate curiosity and adaptive emotional processes and leads to differentiation and adaptive flexibility (Elliott & Greenberg, 2007).

As behavioral therapy and its close affiliate cognitive therapy, as well as humanistic and experiential therapies, arose as challenges to the predominant psychoanalysis, psychoanalysis evolved and modernized as well (Eagle & Wolitzky, 1992; Kernberg, Yeomans, Clarkin, & Levy, 2008; Makari, 2008). Indeed, the modern variations of psychoanalysis are usually referred to as *psychodynamic therapies*. One major deviation from Freudian theory is the object relations school, which emphasizes the human need for attachment to others and the internalization of early attachments.

Therapy is not so much in making the unconscious conscious, but in substituting a good object (i.e., the therapist) for an internalized bad object, such as an unreasonably punitive parent, created in childhood experiences; the therapeutic alliance becomes an important therapeutic vehicle in that process. Rather than interpreting the transference, the therapist responds as a "good object." As the client regresses in therapy, "what needs to be accomplished in treatment is a regression to the point at which these structures developed and *a resumption of developmental growth* [italics added] along new and better pathways" (Eagle & Wolitzky, 1992, p. 132).

Another related thread to modern psychodynamic theory is interpersonal psychotherapy, which emanated from the work of Henry Stack Sullivan. In this thread, relationships with significant others are the vital elements of one's inner world. Anxiety is created in the interpersonal space, initially between infant and mother, but is recreated in repetitive patterns with others as adults. In interpersonal treatments, the observer–therapist is replaced with an interacting therapist: "The therapist is not simply an observer focusing on the patient's predominant modes of interaction, but is an integral part of the interpersonal field as both subject and object" (Eagle & Wolitzky, 1992, p. 134). Klerman and colleagues developed this strand as a focused treatment for depression (Klerman, Weissman, Rounsaville, & Chevron, 1984).

There are a number of important aspects of the development of theoretical models in psychotherapy to keep in mind. First, explanatory models in psychotherapy are decidedly different from those in medicine. Typically in medicine, for a particular disorder, there is a modal explanation for a disorder and one or a few competing treatments based on the modal explanation. In psychotherapy, there is a proliferation of approaches. Most estimates are that there are more than 500 distinct psychotherapy theories and that the number is growing (Kazdin, 2000). Interestingly, many psychotherapeutic theories were originally developed to treat a particular disorder: Psychoanalysis was at its origins a treatment for hysteria, cognitive–behavioral treatment was developed specifically for depression, and behavioral treatments had their roots in the treatment of avoidant types of anxiety. Each of these treatments has expanded and now offers a more general framework for treating a broader range of disorders than originally intended. Many see the multitude of theoretical approaches as a healthy interest in the development of psychotherapy and a pluralistic context that provides a variety of choices for both therapists and clients.

Another consideration is that a compelling case could be made that psychotherapies arise as much or more as a consequence of the cultural context than as a result of the applications of scientific psychology (Engel, 2008; Fancher, 1995; Langman, 1997; Makari, 2008; Pilgram, 1997; Taylor, 1999; Wampold, 2007). Indeed, some have suggested that the power of various approaches to psychotherapy emanates from their acceptability as a healing practice in the society (Anderson, Lunnen, & Ogles, 2010). Psychoanalysis was not simply a practice administered to passive clients; as psychoanalysis gained currency, clients sought it out, which clearly then influenced their expectations about the effectiveness of the treatment.

WINNOWING AND SIFTING THEORIES

The plethora of therapeutic approaches has not resulted in a peaceful coexistence. As was discussed previously, various disciples were expelled from Freud's inner circle because of differences in theory and practice. The behaviorists found the Freudians to be unscientific and were vocal and vociferous critics. For most of the history of psychotherapy, claims of superiority were rhetorical rather than scientific, each proponent claiming superior theory and trotting out dramatic case studies of seemingly miraculous cures. Norcross and Newman (1992) described the situation with great flourish:

> Rivalry among theoretical orientations has a long and undistinguished history in psychotherapy, dating back to Freud. In the infancy of the field, therapy systems, like battling siblings, competed for attention and affection in a "dogma eat dogma" environment. . . . Mutual antipathy and exchange of puerile insults between adherents of rival orientations were much the order of the day. (p. 3)

The proliferation of theoretical approaches posed several particularly troublesome issues for the practice of psychotherapy. First, the contrast between medicine, with seemingly well established explanations and one or a few treatments for each disease, and psychotherapy, with many divergent theories and treatments, was striking and, to many, unsettling. Second, the relation between many of the theories and treatments and psychological science was tenuous. The advocates of some theories took pride in their close association with psychological science (e.g., the behavioral and cognitive therapists), whereas others seemed more distant (e.g., psychoanalytic and humanistic therapists) and still others appeared to be in left field (e.g., thought field therapists; pun intended). Indeed, in 1996, Singer and Lalich (1996) published a book entitled *"Crazy" Therapies* to inform the public about the many therapies they considered to be on the fringe, if not entirely illegitimate. However, as will be discussed, discriminating between legitimate and illegitimate approaches to psychotherapy is a bit tricky— what is the preferred mode of operation to one can be considered a fringe therapy to another (e.g., eye movement desensitization procedures; see Davidson & Parker, 2001; Herbert et al., 2000; F. Shapiro, 1989). A third problem is that a set of more than 500 treatments confuses the public about the nature of psychotherapy and presents problems for the education and training of therapists, as one might well imagine. A fourth problem was that psychotherapy has been fighting to be seen as a recognized treatment within the health care delivery system; an unrestricted variety of treatments, all of which are claimed to be effective, is not particularly appealing to third-party payers, who have limited funds to spend on mental health services.

In the United States, in response to the issues raised by the proliferation of treatments, the Society of Clinical Psychology (Division 12 of the American Psychological Association [APA]) appointed a task force to identify treatments that were scientifically validated (Task Force on Promotion and Dissemination of Psychological Procedures, 1995). The purpose of the project was "to consider methods for educating clinical psychologists, third party payors, and the public about effective psychotherapies" (Task Force on Promotion and Dissemination of Psychological Procedures, 1995, p. 1).

If a treatment satisfied a set of criteria that the Task Force developed, then it was labeled an *empirically validated treatment* (EVT). The initial task force identified 25 treatments that satisfied the criteria, and these treatments were thus referred to as EVTs (Garfield, 1996; Task Force on Promotion and Dissemination of Psychological Procedures, 1995); in 1996, clarifications were made, and the list of EVTs was expanded. Although the Task Force was careful to say that treatments that did not appear on the lists might be efficacious, the endeavor did create a dichotomy: There were treatments that were designated as EVTs, and there were treatments that were not (Garfield, 1996; Henry, 1998; Wampold, 1997; Westen, Novotny, & Thompson-Brenner, 2004). In a very important manner, the EVT project reduced the more than 500 psychotherapies to a small set of psychotherapies (fewer than 50) that had been established by research, primarily clinical trials, to be efficacious. Similar efforts to limit psychotherapy to "scientific approaches" also have been instituted in various countries around the world (e.g., Germany; see Schulte, 2007). Winnowing the glut of psychotherapies by identifying "treatments that work" might appear to be a reasonable and prudent way to proceed. However, the EVT movement generated much criticism and opposition (Garfield, 1996; Henry, 1998; Wampold, 1997; Westen et al., 2004), and the controversy illustrates several of the tensions within the field of psychotherapy.

Essentially, all of the criticisms involve the notion that winnowing the number of psychotherapies privileges those that are contained in the EVT set or other classifications of "scientific" therapies and places those that are not so classified at a disadvantage. Garfield (1996) early on raised the issue about uncertainty in science and the evolving nature of conclusions, expressing concern about whether a treatment can ever be validated. In response to that issue, "validated" was changed to "supported," and in 1998 psychotherapies that met the criteria were labeled *empirically supported treatments* (ESTs).

Several critics have called attention to the close alignment of the EVT/EST project with a medical model of psychotherapy (Garfield, 1996; W. P. Henry, 1998; Messer, 2004; Wampold, 1997, 2001b; Wampold & Bhati, 2004). Indeed, one motivation behind identifying treatments of proved effectiveness was to compete in the health care delivery system: "If clinical psychology is to survive in this heyday of biological psychiatry, APA must act to emphasize the strength of what we have to offer—a variety of psychotherapies of proven efficacy" (Task Force on Promotion and Dissemination of Psychological Procedures, 1995, p. 3). The association with medicine went further, however; the criteria for designating a psychotherapy as an EST were patterned after the Food and Drug Administration (FDA) criteria for approving medications (Wampold, 2001b; Wampold, Lichtenberg, & Waehler, 2002). The criterion stipulating two randomized controlled trials that demonstrate the superiority of the treatment over some type of placebo (either pill or psychological) resembles closely the corresponding FDA requirement for drugs. Indeed, the Task Force was concerned about establishing specificity and patterning the criteria along the lines of medicine:

> We [the Task Force] believe establishing efficacy in contrast to a waiting list control group is not sufficient. Relying on such evidence would leave psychologists at a serious disadvantage vis-à-vis psychiatrists who can point to numerous double-blind placebo trials to support the validity of their interventions. (Task Force on Promotion and Dissemination of Psychological Procedures, 1995, p. 5)

Another observation was that the criteria favored certain types of psychotherapies, which supports the appearance of privilege. Because the criteria stipulated that either clinical trials or replicated single-subject designs were necessary and that all psychotherapies required treatment manuals (Kiesler, 1994), it was argued that behavioral and cognitive–behavioral treatments were advantaged (Garfield, 1996; Henry, 1998; Messer, 2004; Wampold, 1997, 2001b; Wampold & Bhati, 2004) and therapies with more humanistic traditions disadvantaged (Schneider, 2008). Single-subject designs are more appropriate for behavioral interventions than other approaches; manuals are compatible with structured treatments, such as behavioral and cognitive treatments; and clinical trials are expensive, and funding typically has been skewed toward behavioral and cognitive treatments.

Yet another criticism was that the focus of the criteria was on the identification of treatments and thus de-emphasized the common factors among therapies, the therapist, and the context in which treatment was delivered (Garfield, 1996; Henry, 1998; Messer, 2004; Wampold, 1997, 2001a, 2001b; Wampold & Bhati, 2004). In later chapters, evidence will be presented to indicate that the common factors and the context are critical to the success of therapy and that the type of treatment delivered accounts for very little of the variability in outcomes. That is to say, ESTs focus on the treatment when it appears that other variables critical variables are ignored (Wampold, 2001b, 2007).

Despite the issues that have been raised about ESTs, they have undoubtedly had a critical role in publicizing the efficacy of psychotherapy and helped make psychotherapy a legitimate treatment in the health care delivery system of the United States (Barlow, 2004; Wampold, 2007). Nevertheless, the issues raised regarding ESTs are critical to the study of theories of psychotherapy. An orthodox EST stance would focus education and training on those treatments for which there is scientific evidence of efficacy (i.e., ESTs); in this series, a more liberal view is adopted—namely, that many approaches to psychotherapy are legitimate and that scientific evidence supports this more expansive stance.

The effort to update the EST list has waned, and the Task Force has not issued a report since 1996. Nevertheless, the attempt to identify treatments that have empirical support and to differentiate them from other treatments continues. A recent movement in medicine attempts to use research evidence in practice to improve the quality of care. *Evidence-based practice* in medicine "is the integration of best research evidence with clinical expertise and patient values" (Sackett, Straus, Richardson, Rosenberg, & Haynes, 2000, p. 147). Following the medical path, the American Psychological Association adapted the idea of evidence-based practice to psychology by defining evidence-based practice in psychology as "the integration of the best available research with clinical expertise in the context of patient characteristics, culture, and preferences" (APA Presidential Task Force on Evidence-Based Practice, 2006, p. 273). Purposefully, APA took a broad perspective on the nature of evidence:

Best research evidence refers to scientific results related to intervention strategies, assessment, clinical problems, and patient populations in laboratory and field settings as well as to clinically relevant results of basic research in psychology and related fields. APA endorses multiple types of research evidence (e.g., efficacy, effectiveness, cost-effectiveness, cost–benefit, epidemiological, treatment utilization) that contribute to effective psychological practice. (APA Presidential Task Force on Evidence-Based Practice, 2006, p. 274)

APA's policy on evidence-based practice did not endorse the idea of ESTs or any particular system for designating a treatment as privileged by way of the evidence for effectiveness:

The task force did not make specific recommendations about the treatment of particular disorders, nor did it endorse a disorder-specific approach in which a specified and validated treatment designed to treat a specific disorder is to be viewed as *the* appropriate one within the domain of psychological practice. (Wampold, Goodheart, & Levant, 2007, p. 617)

This is important because the term *evidence-based treatment* (EBT) is used to designate treatments for which there is evidence of efficacy (see De Los Reyes & Kazdin, 2008). However, the term is not synonymous with EST in the sense that there are no generally accepted criteria established for EBT and no task force within psychology charged with judging the evidence relative to the criteria (Westen, Novotny, & Thompson-Brenner, 2005), although various systems have been proposed (De Los Reyes & Kazdin, 2008). Most often, the label *EBT* is applied by the advocates of a particular treatment to suggest that the treatment be privileged by virtue of the evidence. Which treatments get designated as having scientific evidence of their effectiveness is partly a matter of history, priorities, and cultural context. For example, in Germany, psychodynamic and cognitive–behavioral treatments are "scientifically recognized" by the Scientific Advisory Board, which is responsible for determining which psychotherapies will be reimbursed (Schulte, 2007).

To this point, the genesis of psychotherapy and various theoretical approaches to psychotherapy have been examined. There are a plethora of approaches, and advocates of these approaches are ardent supporters for their importance, usefulness, and effectiveness; this enthusiasm produces a healthy diversity of theoretical approaches as well as refinement of existing approaches. However, in the 1970s, many developed "a dissatisfaction with single-school approaches and a concomitant desire to look across and beyond school boundaries to see what can learned from other ways of thinking about psychotherapy and change" (Arkowitz, 1992, p. 262). In the next section, these alternatives are briefly discussed.

ALTERNATIVES TO ALLEGIANCE TO A SINGLE THEORY: INTEGRATION, ECLECTICISM, COMMON FACTORS, AND POSTMODERN APPROACHES

Three strategies have been used to move beyond single theoretical approaches: integration, eclecticism, and common factors. As well, the desire to ensure that psychotherapy is effective for and acceptable to various cultural groups has spawned a multicultural counseling and psychotherapy movement, which is an infusion into rather than an integration of various theories.

Theoretical Integration

Theoretical integration is the synthesis of two or more theories into a single conceptualization. The origins of integration have often been traced to Dollard and Miller's (1950) seminal book *Personality and Psychotherapy: An Analysis in Terms of Learning, Thinking, and Culture,* which provided an explanation of neurosis by synthesizing psychoanalysis and behaviorism (Arkowitz, 1992). The treatment offered was a combination of modeling, self-control strategies, and homework assignments, thus introducing behavioral strategies into the psychoanalytic treatment. However, Dollard and Miller's treatment had few adherents, perhaps because both psychoanalysis and behavior therapy retained their orthodoxies and were resistant to the notion of "combining forces" (Arkowitz, 1992; Stricker & Gold, 1996).

The 1960s and 1970s saw a loosening of the rigid boundaries among therapies as psychodynamic therapists became more structured, more attentive to coping strategies in the here and now, and more inclined to assign responsibility to the client (Arkowitz, 1992) and as behavior therapists began to allow mediating constructs, such as cognitions, into their models and to recognize the importance of factors incidental to behavioral theories, such as the therapeutic relationship (Fishman & Franks, 1992). This loosening of boundaries set the stage for Wachtel's (1977) seminal integration of psychoanalysis and behavior therapy, *Psychoanalysis and Behavior Therapy: Toward an Integration*. Wachtel provided an integrated theory of personality and pathology as well as a variety of therapeutic techniques that were consistent with the integration. The essence of Watchel's integration has been summarized by Arkowitz (1992):

> From the psychodynamic perspective, he [Wachtel] emphasized unconscious processes and conflict and the importance of meanings and fantasies that influenced our interactions with the world. From the behavioral side, the elements included the use of active-intervention techniques, a concern with the environmental context of behavior, a focus on the patient's goals in therapy, and a respect for empirical evidence. . . . Active behavioral interventions may also serve as a source of new insights, and insights can promote changes in behavior. (pp. 268–269)

Wachtel's work established the template for theoretical integration in that there existed a set of therapeutic actions that were consistent with the theoretical synthesis (Stricker & Gold, 1996). Wachtel's work not only provided a hybrid model but also influenced the manner in which behavior therapy and psychodynamic therapies were practiced—psychodynamic therapy became more focused on discrete goals and actions to reach those goals, and behavior therapists were given permission to conceptualize cases in psychodynamic terms.

Since Wachtel's seminal work, psychotherapy integration has grown in terms of the number of integrations and in terms of the interest shown by academics and practitioners (Wampold, 2005), as evidenced by two handbooks on the topic (Norcross & Goldfried, 1992, 2005). Theoretical integration, as a movement, must grapple with several issues (Arkowitz, 1992; Wampold, 2005). There is the risk that an integration becomes yet another theoretical approach in its own right, adding to the expanding number of therapies. As well, most current psychotherapies, while having names that imply purity, are amalgamations of various theoretical perspectives and techniques. For example, cognitive–behavioral therapy is an integration of cognitive principles into a behavioral framework (Fishman & Franks, 1992). Various mindfulness techniques have been integrated into CBT (e.g., dialectical behavior therapy; Linehan et al., 2006). The integrative models raise interesting research issues: If an integrative treatment is found to be efficacious, then it is unclear whether (a) it is any more efficacious than the pure treatments on which it is based and (b) the benefits are due to the integration or to one or more of the various components. Nevertheless, theoretical integration is attractive to many therapists who find "one true light" restricting and who have divergent theoretical curiosity; clients as well can appreciate and benefit from the flexibility.

Technical Eclecticism

Sounds like a logical approach

In 1969, Paul asked the question, "What treatment, by whom, is most effective for this individual with that specific problem, under which set of circumstances, and how does it come about?" (p. 111). Technical eclecticism approaches psychotherapy by attempting to answer Paul's question by identifying the optimal approach for each client based on the disorder, characteristics of the client, and the context in which the problem occurs. In technical eclecticism, the search for the optimal intervention is empirically driven, and theory becomes relatively unimportant. The two most conspicuous systems for technical eclecticism are Arnold Lazarus's multimodal therapy (see, e.g., Lazarus, 1981) and Larry Beutler's systematic eclectic psychotherapy (see, e.g., Beutler & Clarkin, 1990). Although both of these approaches have social learning theory as a base, they are not limited to any techniques from that approach. An example of a prescription of technical eclecticism is the recommendation that clients who are characteristically resistant to advice or suggestion (have a high reactance potential) would benefit most from relatively unstructured treatments (Beutler, Harwood, Alimohamed, & Malik, 2002).

why?

Is this the placebo effect?

Common Factors

Under frequent discussion in recent years is the concept of *common factors,* or the idea that aspects of treatment that were common to various therapies may be responsible for successful treatment, as opposed to factors specifically associated with a particular therapy. Common factors are those aspects of treatment that are present in most or all psychotherapies, such as a relationship with an empathic therapist, a client seeking treatment for distress, a treatment structure, and the creation of hope. As contemporary as the concept of common factors seems, it has its roots in the early 20th century. As early as the 1930s, an increase in the number of psychotherapies was evident. The orthodoxy of psychoanalysis gave way to variation as approaches were offered by neo-Freudians such as Karen Horney, Alfred Adler, Carl Jung, and Harry Stack Sullivan (Cushman, 1992). At the same time, Christian Science remained a popular faith-based psychological intervention. Claims of treatment success were critical to the vitality of the relatively young profession, and with each approach advocates saw remarkable benefits accrue. This, of course, reinforced the notion that each of the treatments was effective because of the unique and potent actions of the therapists who adhered to the protocols.

In the 1930s, Rosenzweig (1936) presciently observed that perhaps the benefits of the various psychotherapies were due to some aspects of therapy common to all approaches, a view that represented theoretical heresy! Rosenzweig proposed that all approaches provided by a competent therapist who believed in the treatment would result in about the same outcome, and thus the particular approach was not critical:

> The proud proponent, having achieved success in the cases he mentions, implies, even when he does not say it, that his ideology is thus proved true, all others false. . . . [However,] it is soon realized that besides the intentionally utilized methods and their consciously held theoretical foundations, there are inevitably certain *unrecognized factors* in any therapeutic situation—factors that may be even more important than those being purposely employed. (p. 412)

Rosenzweig (1936) used an *Alice in Wonderland* metaphor to refer to the equivalence in outcomes: "At last the Dodo said, 'Everybody has won, and all must have prizes'" (p. 412). The metaphor persisted, thanks to a seminal article by Luborsky, Singer, and Luborsky (1975), which used the phrase as a subtitle and provided research evidence that perhaps Rosenzweig was correct. The allusion persisted, and today the equivalence of treatments is simply called the *dodo bird effect*. The empirical evidence for this counterintuitive idea is discussed later in this volume (see chap. 4).

The common factor notion gained some popularity in the 1960s, most notably through the work of Jerome Frank, as described in his seminal book *Persuasion and Healing* (Frank & Frank, 1991). Frank's model, which is actually a transcultural model of healing practices, of which psychotherapy would be a special case (Wampold, 2007), involved four components. The first component is an emotionally charged and confiding relationship between the healer (i.e., the therapist in psychotherapy) and the client. The second is the context of the practice, in which the healer is given special status and perceived to have powers to heal. In the case of psychotherapy, the therapist is a professional (i.e., has training, degrees, and credentials) and is perceived to be effective by the client and to work in the client's best interests.

The third component is that the actions of the healer have a rationale that is cogent and powerful to the client. The rationale, according to Frank and others (Wampold, 2007), need not be scientifically sound, and he consequently substituted the term *myth* for rationale—what is important is that the explanation for the client's distress be accepted by the client and lead to a solution to the presenting problem (Wampold, 2007; Wampold, Imel, Bhati, & Johnson Jennings, 2006). In psychotherapy, the rationale or myth is the theoretical model used by the therapist.

The fourth and final component is a treatment, which Frank called the *procedure* or *ritual*. Every psychotherapy has a set of procedures that is consistent with the rationale of the treatment. Psychodynamic therapists make interpretations, experiential therapists facilitate the exploration of feelings and experiences in the here and now, cognitive therapists assist the client in changing irrational or maladaptive cognitions, and behavioral therapists create opportunities to expose the client to feared stimuli, for example.

Is this not stating the obvious?.

might as well talk to a mind

In Frank's model, the presence of a cogent theory and rationale and a treatment that is consistent with that rationale are common factors; consequently, any procedure that lacks these elements does not contain essential aspects of psychotherapy. In various clinical trials of psychotherapy, control conditions have consisted of *treatment conditions* in which the client meets with a therapist and the therapist responds to the client and may reflect the client's emotions, but no treatment rationale exists and no therapeutic actions, as therapist would know them, are delivered. According to Frank's model, such a condition would not contain all of the common factors and indeed would lack two of the most important common factors: rationale (myth) and treatment (ritual). Rationale and treatment are critical in understanding the evidence for how psychotherapy works.

Since Rosenzweig (1936) proposed that common elements of therapy were responsible for the benefits of psychotherapy, attempts have been made to identify and codify the aspects of therapy common to all psychotherapies. Goldfried (1980) discussed the strategy level of abstraction, between techniques and theoretical orientation, and suggested that examination at this level might produce common principles of change. He suggested two possible principles that are common to all therapies: providing the client new and corrective experiences and offering the client direct feedback. Castonguay (1993) noted that focusing on therapist actions, such as therapeutic strategies, ignored other common aspects of psychotherapy. He distinguished three meanings that can be applied to understanding common factors in psychotherapy. The first meaning, which is similar to Goldfried's strategy level of abstraction, refers to global aspects of therapy that are not specific to any one approach (i.e., are common across approaches), such as insight, corrective experiences, opportunity to express emotions, and acquisition of a sense of mastery. The second meaning pertains to aspects of treatment that are auxiliary to treatment and refers primarily to the interpersonal and social factors. This second meaning encompasses the therapeutic context and the therapeutic relationship (e.g., the working alliance). The third meaning of the term involves those aspects of the treatment that influence outcomes but that are not therapeutic activities or related to the interpersonal/social context. This latter meaning includes client expectancies and involvement in the therapeutic process.

Recognizing that lists of common factors could be generated with relative ease, researchers attempted to bring a conceptual scheme to the common factors. Grencavage and Norcross (1990) reviewed publications that discussed commonalities among therapies and segregated commonalities into five areas: client characteristics, therapist qualities, change processes, treatment structures, and relationship elements. Lambert (1992) parsed the various factors that led to psychotherapy success into four categories, in order of their importance for producing therapeutic benefits: (a) client/extracurricular factors; (b) relationship factors; (c) placebo, hope, and expectancy factors; and (d) model/technique factors. According to Lambert, the most important factor, client/extracurricular factors, involves characteristics of the client and events that occur outside of therapy. Quite clearly, much of what happens in therapy is due to the client's motivation, resources (e.g., social support), and personality structure as well as to events that transpire indirectly as a result of therapy (e.g., a depressed husband talks to his wife about his distress) or serendipitously (e.g., a client's parent dies unexpectedly). The second most important aspect, according to Lambert, involves relationship factors, which include all of the aspects of being in a relationship with a genuine, empathic, and caring therapist who facilitates work toward solving problematic issues. The third factor, placebo, hope, and expectancy, is created as function of seeking help from a professional in the healing context—the client believes that the therapy will helpful. Finally, according to Lambert, model/technique factors account for part of the success of psychotherapy. That is to say, the ingredients of the specific treatment are responsible for the some of the benefits of psychotherapy. A popular book titled *Heart and Soul of Change* (Hubble, Duncan, & Miller, 1999a) was organized around Lambert's categories (Hubble, Duncan, & Miller, 1999b) and promoted the power of the common factors.

One of the problems with the various discussions of common factors is that the factors are either listed singly or categorized into subsets, as if these common factors were ingredients to be added to the pot. However, Frank's (Frank & Frank, 1991) model is an integrated model that explained how the various common factors fit together to constitute a healing practice, similar to traditional healing practices throughout human civilizations (Wampold, 2007). Other variations of integrated models have been offered, notably by Orlinsky and Howard (1986), Weinberger and colleagues (Weinberger, Rasco, & Hofmann, 2007) and Wampold and colleagues (Imel & Wampold, 2008; Wampold, 2001b, 2007).

Postmodern Developments

Postmodern philosophy, although complex and not well defined, embraces several notions that have been incorporated into recent psychotherapy theory. Postmodernism recognizes that history, ethics, morals, and social science are created within the context of social interaction, that much of what is taken for granted is actually socially constructed, that power shapes what is taken for "truth," and that new constructions are needed to negotiate the propinquity of cultures.

One of the perspectives of psychotherapy that could be said to emanate from postmodernism is multicultural counseling and psychotherapy. Multicultural theories challenge the notion that people can be treated for mental disorders that reside in the mind and suggest instead that cultural considerations, both in the manifestation of problems and in their treatment, must be central (Coleman & Wampold, 2003; Gielen, Draguns, & Fish, 2008; Gielen, Fish, & Draguns, 2004). This notion is incompatible in many ways with the development of particular treatments for particular disorders, particularly those that posit an intrapsychic locus of the problem and ignore cultural influences. In the United States and many other countries, the increasing diversity of residents makes the multicultural perspective an imperative. For example, in the United States, surveys indicate that racial and ethnic minorities receive less mental health services than European Americans (Wang et al., 2005), despite demonstrated need. Individuals with low incomes, members of racial and ethnic minorities, immigrants, and other groups (e.g., gay men and lesbians) experience considerable stress emanating from social forces (Williams, Neighbors, & Jackson, 2008).

Several psychotherapy theorists noted early on that psychotherapy shared many similarities with ethnocultural healing (e.g., Jerome Frank, as early as 1961). Although these conceptualizations considered the role of culture, they did not contain an explicit recognition of the issues involved in the delivery of mental health services to racial and ethnic minority groups. In 1962, C. Gilbert Wrenn, in a prescient discussion of the coming diversification of the population, authored the book *Counselor in a Changing World*. He coined the term *culturally encapsulated counselor* to describe a therapist who is unable to understand that the culture of the client, which in a changing world could well be very different from that of the therapist, is critical to effective therapy. As described by Pedersen (2001), "Culturally encapsulated counselors disregard cultural variations and impose their own self-reference criteria, implicit assumptions disregarding reasonable proof and/or rational consistency, simplistic technique-oriented solutions applied to complex problems, and the dominant culture values as universals" (pp. 16–17). Although Pedersen recognized that there were other claimants of the title "fourth force" (after psychoanalytic, behavioral, and humanistic approaches), Pedersen made the claim that multicultural approaches to psychotherapy were entitled to assume a prominent place in the theoretical landscape (Pedersen, 1990, 2001). Pedersen and others have gone further to suggest that all psychotherapy is cultural—the therapist and the client are each thickly embedded in their cultures, and all therapy negotiates— or, more strongly, uses—these cultural values.

In some ways, multicultural counseling and therapy is not a theoretical approach but an imperative to adapt or develop treatments that are effective for and acceptable to clients of all groups. In the latter decades of the 20th century, concerted efforts were made to understand the dynamics involved in providing services to individuals diverse in terms of race, ethnicity, culture, acculturation, sexual identity, socioeconomic status, and physical abilities, among others (Comas-Diaz, 2000; Hall, 2001; Ponterotto, Casas, Suzuki, & Alexander, 1995; Sue, 1998; Sue & Lam, 2002; Sue, Zane, & Young, 1994; Zane, Sue, Young, Nunez, & Hall, 2004).

In 2003, the American Psychological Association (APA) published a policy that enunciated guidelines for psychologists engaging in education, training, research, and practice. These guidelines emphasize three aspects important for the cultural competence of psychotherapists: knowledge, awareness, and skills. *Knowledge* includes knowledge of other cultures as

[handwritten margin note: yes, because you cannot separate a client from his culture. It is an integral part of who he is.]

well as knowledge of self. The interaction of the culture of the therapist and the culture of the client was recognized in the APA principles of evidence-based practice: "Psychologists understand how their own characteristics, values, and context interact with those of the client" (APA Presidential Task Force on Evidence-Based Practice, 2006, p. 284). *Awareness* is the ability to understand interactions from one's own culture and the culture of the client. *Skills* involve the competence to respond appropriately and effectively with clients of a variety of cultures.

There is interest in whether treatments whose efficacy in clinical trials conducted with primarily European American clients can be "exported" to culturally different clients (Coleman & Wampold, 2003; Gielen et al., 2008). One perspective is that best practices (i.e., the best treatment available) should be used with all people until such time as there is empirical evidence that a particular treatment is superior to another for a particular population. A second perspective posits that existing treatments should be adapted for particular populations; that is, Treatment A should be delivered in a culturally sensitive way to a certain cultural group. The third perspective is that all treatments are culturally embedded and that culturally specific treatments should be developed de novo for various cultural groups. There are some fundamental issues inherent in these three options, and clearly the research evidence is insufficient to declare which of them will produce the greatest benefit for various cultural groups (Coleman & Wampold, 2003).

Feminist therapy (see, e.g., Brown, 2006; Evans, Kincade, Marbley, & Seem, 2005) has many similarities to multicultural therapy and could be thought of as emanating from postmodern philosophy as well. Feminist therapy recognizes that gender roles, gender role status, attitudes toward women, social norms, and other social, cultural, and legal mores related to women create disadvantages. Moreover, these social constructs are intricately woven into the fabric of women's well-being—and many would contend into the fabric of men's well-being as well. Feminist therapy involves empowerment and egalitarianism and eschews intrapsychic causes of distress, and it is effectively applied with both male and female clients (for more information, see the book on feminist therapy in this series; Brown, 2009).

THE BASICS OF PSYCHOTHERAPY

Another therapy that is related to postmodernism as well as the humanistic tradition is narrative therapy (Angus & McCloud, 2007). Narrative therapy posits that people's identity is formed from the stories they create and tell about their lives—that is, one's narratives are shaped by, but also shape, one's self in context. Client problems are part of the narrative, but the focus is on the meaning of one's stories and not on the problems as entities. The process of therapy changes meanings that are ascribed to various aspects of one's life, including one's challenges.

CONCLUSION

Psychotherapy originated in the United States in an unusual combination of religion, psychology, and medicine. The talking cure existed when Freud introduced psychoanalysis to America in his lectures at Clark University at the beginning of the 20th century. Psychoanalysis offered a cogent psychological explanation for mental disorders and their treatment. However, the primacy of psychoanalytic perspectives was challenged first by behavioral approaches and then by humanistic approaches. Confusing the theoretical landscape were efforts to integrate theories, the emergence of eclecticism, and claims that the commonalities of treatments were more important than the specific ingredients. Finally, a recognition that psychotherapy needed to adapt to various cultural groups made the landscape even more complex. Efforts have been made to identify some treatments as being superior to others to reduce the complexity and provide clinicians with recommended treatments. One of these efforts was based on the identification of treatments that have sufficient evidence to indicate that they are effective.

3

The Role of Theory

Psychotherapy theories are explanations of human functioning and the process of change. As the previous chapters have illustrated, there is a wide variety of psychotherapy theories, creating vociferous debates about the advantages and disadvantages of particular theories. However, such debates obscure the importance of theory—any theory—in the process and outcome of psychotherapy. To understand the role of theory in therapy, it is important to keep in mind Frank's *common factors* in therapy (Frank & Frank, 1991): (a) an emotionally charged and confiding relationship between the healer and the client, (b) a healer who is given special status and is perceived to have the powers to heal, (c) a powerful and cogent rationale for the healer's actions, and (d) a set of treatment actions that are consistent with the rationale. These components are vacuous without theory—simply, there is no therapy without theory. Every client wants an explanation for what ails him or her and a set of therapeutic actions that the client believes will improve his or her condition. The last two components— the rationale and the treatment—emanate necessarily from theory. The therapist needs to have a deep understanding of theory and to be able to communicate it convincingly to the client.

In this chapter, several aspects of psychotherapy theories are discussed. First, the nature of theories in psychotherapy is explained to answer the question, What are psychotherapy theories? Next, the importance of theory for the therapist and for the client is discussed. Then, some philosophical issues are presented that reveal some insights into the arguments about what are "preferred" theories.

WHAT ARE THE ELEMENTS OF
A PSYCHOTHERAPY THEORY?

It is clear at this point that there are many psychotherapy theories, that they were spawned from different philosophies of science, and that they differ in many important ways. Despite this divergence, there are structural similarities, as the theories address similar questions, albeit with different answers. In this section, the major questions that most theories answer are described. It may be the case that various theories do not address these questions explicitly, but digging a bit below the surface makes it clear that the theories have these questions at their core.

The first question that each theory addresses is, What is the core motivation of human existence? For example, are humans motivated to action by instinctual and biological drives? Or is the motivation interpersonal and relational in nature? Will people always tend toward "good or evil"? Are we "blank slates" on which life lessons are written? Do we respond primarily to the environment, or are we agentic?

Many of these types of questions can be boiled down to two fundamental questions: What are the characteristics of a healthy personality? and How does psychopathology develop? In one respect, these questions are innately developmental—What happens to the human organism that derails healthy development? This question raises the further issue of "nurture versus nature." From the former perspective, one can ask about critical developmental stages and events that occur to thwart normal development. From the latter perspective, one is interested in the environmental events that lead to an expression of the gene that results in manifest pathology.

All theories, to a greater or lesser extent, are interested in the role social relations play in the healthy personality and in dysfunction. Some theories place more emphasis on early social attachments, mainly with parents, whereas others examine current social support and social relations. A related question is whether problems exist within the individual or are created in the social milieu (e.g., by a dysfunctional family). Both

An additional set of differences occur as theories place emphasis on various systems to the exclusion of others. Thus, various theories emphasize affect, cognition, or behavior. It might be said that theories are not so much different from each other, but rather place relative emphases on particular systems. Other theories may eschew a focus on organismic systems and focus instead on social systems; these theories, for example, would address how culture influences human functioning, particularly psychological well-being and dysfunction.

Needless to say, there are a myriad of questions that theories address and many ways to think about the similarities and differences among theories. One scheme for examining these issues is presented in Table 3.1, where the four major forces of psychotherapy discussed previously are presented along with six particular issues: (a) the philosophy of science from which the theories emanate, (b) the perspective taken on human motivation, (c) the perspective taken on human development, (d) the definition of psychological health, (e) the therapeutic stance and roles of the therapist and the client, and (f) the manner in which the goals and outcomes of therapy are framed (Murdock, 2008). This table provides a schema that will help readers understand the various theories as they are presented in the books that follow.

ROLE OF THEORY FOR THERAPISTS

For the therapist, the theory becomes the map for psychotherapy. A map is only a pictorial presentation of the geographic/political/economic space with various delineated routes from one location to another. There are many maps to choose from—road maps, satellite views, topographical maps, climate maps, political maps, economic maps, and so forth. None of

Table 3.1

Components of Major Psychotherapy Theories

Theory	Philosophy of science	Human motivation	Human development	Psychological health	Therapeutic stance	Goals/outcomes
Psychoanalytic/ psychodynamic	Positivist/realist	Pessimistic to neutral; must overcome instinctual urges and early life experiences	Psychosexual stages of development; early attachment experiences critical	Healthy defenses, sufficient ego strength, secure attachment style	Formal therapist/ patient roles	Personality change, resolution of unconscious conflicts, insight, integration
Cognitive/ behavioral	Positivist/post-positivist	Neutral; humans adapt to environment	Learning paramount, shaped by experience	Adaptive behavior, adaptive cognitions, absence of dysfunction	Teacher, consultant	Distress reduction, symptom reduction, adaptive functioning
Humanistic/ existential	Phenomenological	Some optimistic (tendency to self-actualize); some negative to neutral (existential search for meaning)	Not explicit	Authenticity, congruence, awareness, acceptance of self and others	Authentic and present in the here and now	Authenticity, freedom, understanding, meaningful existence, self-actualization
Multicultural/ feminist/narrative	Postmodern	Ambiguous; search for meaning, exertion of power	Context (culture, gender, power) critical	Empowered, meaningful life, unconstrained by power and isms (e.g., racism)	Egalitarian, collaborative	Empowerment; reduction of barriers, oppression, and privilege; opportunity to achieve life goals

these maps is "reality," but each *represents* phenomena in a useful way. Some are more useful for some purposes (e.g., driving) than others (e.g., hiking). Psychotherapy theory provides a map for the therapist—not a complete reflection of reality, but a useful representation. Each psychotherapy theory gives the therapist an idea of the "lay of the land" and helps him or her get from Point A to Point B. In psychotherapy language, the theory provides the basis for case conceptualization and treatment planning. *Case conceptualization* describes the nature of the psychological problem and dysfunction within the theoretical framework chosen by the therapist. *Treatment planning* involves how the therapist plans to work with the client to remediate the client's difficulties. In a way, conceptualization and treatment planning involve explanation and action, two critical components of psychotherapy (Frank & Frank, 1991; Wampold, 2007).

The theory provides the structure for case conceptualization, but the data are provided by the client, either directly (e.g., in the clinical interview) or indirectly (e.g., via material in the client's chart or information from assessment procedures). Some therapists rely solely on the clinical interview for data, and others administer various assessment instruments. Even the choice of assessment instruments reflects theory, as a cognitive–behavioral therapist might use a symptom-focused measure whereas the psychodynamic therapist might use a projective test. Regardless, these data are filtered through the theoretical lens—data without inference have no meaning to the therapist. Of course, any explanation of the client's problem should be considered tentative, and the therapist should be open to disconfirming the conclusions reached. Disconfirming evidence need not result in abandonment of the theory, but perhaps only a reformulation within the theory. In a sense, continuing the map metaphor, the map has to be revised as the journey progresses. Of course, the skilled therapist also integrates the best research evidence about the client's disorder or problems and their treatment, as well as the client's characteristics, context, and preferences (APA Presidential Task Force on Evidence-Based Practice, 2006).

Given the variety of psychotherapy theories, which should the therapist choose? This choice is influenced by a variety of intersecting forces but is guided by an overarching consideration: What theory will best help this particular client? The answer to this question is interminable—simply said, it is not possible to say with certainty which theory would benefit the client the most. Yet there are many essential considerations when choosing a theory, as a lifelong pursuit and for a particular client.

Most important, the therapist and the theory must be compatible. Therapists are attracted to therapies that they find comfortable, interesting, and, attractive. Comfort most likely derives from the similarity between the worldview of the theory and the attitudes and values of the therapist. A perusal of Table 3.1 reveals a broad range of very basic values, say in terms of psychological health. Comfort, however, is also derived from the interpersonal demands inherent in the therapy. For example, some theories depend on the presence of the therapist in the here and now more than others; some therapists, because of their interpersonal skills and personality, are more comfortable with the intense emotional encounters inherent in such therapies. Other therapists may be more comfortable with the teacher/consultant role of behavioral treatments (see Table 3.1). Interest in the therapy may also come from its intellectual aspects; reading psychodynamic theories is a much different experience than reading behavioral theories. Some theories are more reductionistic and pragmatic, whereas others are more philosophical and abstract; a theory that is attractive to one person will turn off another. This is not, most likely, a scholarly calculus, in which one catalogues what is attractive about the various theories, but rather a visceral reaction—as you read this series, you will find yourself nodding in approval and enthusiasm for some of the theories, whereas others might bore you or even anger you. Interestingly, good theories make good reading: In three surveys about "great books" in psychology, Norcross and Tomcho (1994) found that many of the top-rated authors were psychotherapy theorists (viz., Freud, Rogers, Erikson).

A second consideration, not unrelated to the first, is that the therapist must believe that the theory, as implemented by himself or herself, will be effective. A few subtleties here are worth pondering. As discussed previously, some consider evidence-based treatments (EBTs) or empirically supported treatments (ESTs) more effective than other treatments, whereas others might say that although perhaps it has not been proved that EBTs and ESTs are more effective, they are clearly preferred because evidence exists that they are effective. But, as discussed in chapter 4, such claims ignore an important aspect related to the delivery of psychotherapy—namely, the therapist! In the clinical trials that produce the evidence, the ESTs or EBTs typically are delivered by therapists who have an allegiance to the treatment. These trials do not have much to say about the effectiveness of ESTs or EBTs delivered by those who do not find them appealing. Indeed, there is research that shows that allegiance to the treatment is related to outcome (see chaps. 4 and 5). There is also conclusive evidence that much of the variability in outcomes is due to the therapist (Kim, Wampold, & Bolt, 2006; Wampold, 2006; Wampold & Brown, 2005). Therefore, it makes little sense to discuss the effectiveness of a particular treatment without considering who is giving the treatment (for a discussion of this issue, see Elkin, 1999). Thus, the question, Which treatment will be most effective? is incomplete. The better question is, Which treatment delivered by me will be most effective? The answer to the latter question is much more complex but has much to do with attraction to the therapy—therapists providing a treatment that they find interesting and compatible will likely be more effective than therapists delivering a treatment not to their liking.

A further subtlety is centered on the idea of belief in a treatment. One interpretation of the term *belief* is that it connotes a conviction that the theory is a true explanation of the client's dysfunction. According to this interpretation, belief is derived from the "truthiness"[1] of the theory; some theories are more valid explanations for psychological dysfunction and its remediation than others. Such claims are philosophically and empirically problematic—simply, as is discussed in this chapter and the next two, no theory is clearly more truthful than another (for a discussion of this issue, see Wampold, Imel, Bhati, & Johnson Jennings, 2006). This raises a thorny question: How does one have belief in a theory if the truthiness of the

---

[1]The term *truthiness* is used to avoid complex philosophical issues related to the concept of truth. Some of these philosophical ideas are considered briefly later in this chapter.

theory cannot be established, philosophically or empirically? The resolution ironically is subtly simple: The belief that the therapist must have is that the treatment, as delivered by him or her, will be effective. This is different than the belief that the treatment is the most effective, most truthful, most useful, most efficient, or best in any other way.

A third consideration when choosing a theory is related to mastery. To be effective, a therapist practices and continually improves, learning initially from master therapists. In many ways, one learns psychotherapy at the foot of a master (Orlinsky & Ronnestad, 2005). Therapists in training have limited opportunities to learn various therapies and therefore are restricted to learning theories for which there are expert instructors and supervisors. It is awfully difficult, if not impossible, to learn a theory on one's own. And, as discussed in the next section, it is recommended that therapists not be restricted to a single theoretical approach. There is some wisdom in learning some treatments that one may not prefer as well as one's preferred theory, particularly if there are master therapists available. Although workshops, video materials, and other resources are extremely valuable, it is wise to learn as much about particular theories as one can from local master therapists, supervisors, and clinical instructors, regardless of whether the theories espoused by these trainers are perfect matches for the trainee.

The fourth consideration when choosing a theory is related to eclecticism and theory integration (Arkowitz, 1992; Garfield, 1992; Norcross & Goldfried, 2005; Orlinsky & Ronnestad, 2005). It is quite rare that therapists choose only one theory because, as stated above, no one theory successfully explains entirely human nature and behavior, mental health, or mental disorder. Therapists may very well find that their visceral response to the theories presented encompasses two, three, or more different theories. Indeed, about a third of practicing psychologists indicate that their approach is eclectic or integrationist (Norcross, Hedges, & Castle, 2002). The key to adopting an eclectic theoretical framework is to develop a coherent, integrated, and strategic approach to healing. For example, a therapist may hold that humans are inherently "good" and, given the right circumstances, will flourish; that suffering is an integral part of existence;

that knowledge is best gained through deep understanding of others' subjective reality; that systems such as families, societies, and cultures shape
our personalities; that humans, although ultimately alone, live in relation
to others; that humans are biological and instinctual beings and learn
throughout their lifetime; and that affect, cognition, and behavior are
intertwined. Obviously, it is impossible to choose one theory that encapsu-
lates all of these belief systems. It is possible to conceptualize a case psycho-
dynamically and intervene cognitively, as long as the treatment makes
sense to the client, is accepted by the client, and leads to client progress.

ROLE OF THEORY FOR THE CLIENT

To this point, the discussion has focused on the role of the therapist in
selecting a theory. However, the theory is also important to the client,
albeit in a very different way. Typically, clients come to psychotherapy
when their own efforts have been inadequate to overcome their difficulties and they believe that despite their best efforts, their distress will continue. That is, their explanation for their disorders provides little hope for
change. Clients may attribute their difficulties to internal factors over
which they have no control (i.e., they are unintelligent) or external factors
arrayed against them (people have treated them poorly and will do so in
the future). A potent aspect of psychotherapy is that it provides an adaptive explanation—one that gives clients the expectation that their selves
are not immutable and their problems are not inevitable (Frank & Frank,
1991; Wampold, 2007). Of course, each theory tells the story differently—
irrational thoughts, unconscious motivations, unexpressed emotions, poor
attachment histories—but each tells a hopeful story to the client: "If you
believe in this new explanation and follow the steps in this treatment, your
problems will be manageable and life will be better." In common factor
models, acquisition of adaptive explanations is central to change in psychotherapy (Anderson et al., 2010; Frank & Frank, 1991; Imel & Wampold,
2008; Wampold, Imel, et al., 2006).

Humans strive for understanding, and all healing practices provide an
explanation in the language of the practice (e.g., medical explanations are

biochemical). Yalom (1995) succinctly summarized the importance of explanation:

> The unexplained—especially the fearful unexplained—cannot be tolerated for long. All cultures, through either a scientific or a religious explanation, attempt to make sense of chaotic and threatening situations. . . . One of our chief methods of control is through language. Giving a name to chaotic, unruly forces provides us with a sense of mastery or control. (p. 84)

Explanation itself is not sufficient, however. The actions of specific therapies are essential as well, as they assist in the induction of belief in the explanation and promote an important set of healthy actions (Wampold, 2007). Belief in an adaptive explanation and healthy actions in therapy have been characterized in different ways by different theorists, using different, but related, constructs such as remoralization, mastery, self-efficacy, change in response expectancies, and so forth (Wampold, 2007). This is all to say that the explanation provided by the therapist and acquired by the client is central to the process of psychotherapy, and this explanation is derived from the psychotherapy theory, again illustrating the quintessential role of psychotherapy theory.

The role of theory has several aspects that are vital for the client. The issue of truthiness must be addressed here as well. As was the case for the therapist, the scientific validity of a theory is subsidiary to its utility for the client. If the explanation is cogent, is acceptable, creates positive expectations, and leads to healthy action, then it will likely be beneficial to the client. Indeed, the exact nature of the explanation, as understood by the therapist, is not what is communicated to the client. Just as medical doctors do not provide detailed biochemical explanations to patients, therapists do not provide detailed psychological explanations. Rather, therapists provide explanations that are understandable and persuasive. Indeed, the explanation does not necessarily even have to be consistent with the theory the therapist is using, although usually it is. Again, therapists are less concerned with the scientific validity of theory than they are with the impact of the explanation on the client, a point fully recognized by Donald Meichenbaum, a prominent cognitive–behavioral therapist and scientist:

> As part of the therapy rationale, the therapist conceptualized each client's anxiety in terms of Schacter's model of emotional arousal. . . . After laying this groundwork, the therapist noted that the patient's fear seemed to fit Schacter's theory that an emotional state such as fear is in large part determined by the thoughts in which the client engages when physically aroused. . . . Although the theory and research upon which it is based have been criticized . . . the theory has an aura of plausibility that the clients tend to accept: The logic of the treatment plan is clear to clients in light of this conceptualization. (Meichenbaum, 1986, p. 370)

An interesting coda to this discussion is that therapists, when seeking their own personal therapy, often do not select therapists of the same orientation as their own (Bike, Norcross, & Schatz, 2009; Norcross, Bike, & Evans, 2009), demonstrating a willingness to be theoretically flexible and not fastidiously invested in one true theory.

A critical aspect of the change process is the acceptance of the explanation provided by the therapist. The explanation should be compatible with the attitudes and values of the client. If not, the client is likely to resist the explanation. This consideration converges with the notions of culturally sensitive treatments that are discussed in the multicultural counseling literature (Atkinson, Bui, & Mori, 2001; Atkinson, Worthington, & Dana, 1991; Coleman & Wampold, 2003). Certain types of clients are more prone to accept and benefit from certain types of treatments. For example, clients who are characteristically resistant benefit more from less structured treatments (Beutler, Moleiro, & Talebi, 2002), clients who are not ready to change respond poorly to therapists who impose action or premature change (Prochaska & Norcross, 2002), and clients do best when the internality or externality of the treatment matches the internality or externality of their avoidance styles (Beutler, Harwood, Alimohamed, & Malik, 2002).

Acceptance is also influenced by the person of the therapist. If the therapist is seen as a trusted healer, is persuasive, and works collaboratively with the client, the likelihood that the client will accept the offered explanation and will be more engaged in the therapy is greater (Wampold, 2007). Effective therapists are quite persuasive when it comes to encouraging clients that a particular approach will be helpful (Goates-Jones & Hill, 2008). It appears that clients pick therapists on the basis of personal characteristics such as reliability, warmth, empathy, and competence rather than on the basis of theoretical orientation (Bike et al., 2009; Norcross et al., 2009; Wampold, 2001b).

What seems clear is that if a client is not attuned to the approach being offered and shows resistance to the treatment, persistently and insistently offering the same approach is not therapeutically helpful and probably is harmful (Henry, Schacht, Strupp, Butler, & Binder, 1993; Henry, Strupp, Butler, Schacht, & Binder, 1993). On the other hand, either not providing a cogent explanation to the client or providing a confusing explanation is not therapeutic either. Indeed, research indicates that the purity of treatment is related to outcome (Luborsky, McLellan, Diguer, Woody, & Seligman, 1997; Luborsky, McLellan, Woody, O'Brien, & Auerbach, 1985), suggesting that indeed a coherent framework needs to be communicated to clients. This idea of "purity of treatment" should not be understood as slavish adherence to one theory and one theory only, however.

With regard to the client, it appears that a cogent, acceptable, and adaptive explanation must be present. Acceptance is based on the manner in which it is offered and the characteristics and context of the clients. When it appears that the client is not accepting a treatment, either the treatment should be modified or another treatment should be used. This leads to the wise advice of Jerome Frank:

> My position is not that technique is irrelevant to outcome. Rather, I maintain that . . . the success of all techniques depends on the patient's sense of alliance with an actual or symbolic healer. This position implies that ideally therapists should select for each patient the therapy that accords, or can be brought to accord, with the patient's personal characteristics and view of the problem. Also implied is that therapists should seek to learn as many approaches

as they find congenial and convincing. Creating a good therapeutic match may involve both educating the patient about the therapist's conceptual scheme and, if necessary, modifying the scheme to take into account the concepts the patient brings to therapy. (Frank & Frank, 1991, p. xv) *The approach needs to be as individualized as the client.*

THEORY AND PHILOSOPHY OF SCIENCE

The discussion of the role of theory for the therapist and for the client has skirted the issue of how theory and science are related, a topic that is embedded in the philosophy of science and that many clinicians (and many researchers, for that matter) tend to avoid. The philosophical bases of theories were briefly discussed in chapter 2, but the importance of the philosophy of science considerations is illustrated by examining Table 3.1.

At the dawn of the Enlightenment, there was a rejection of the metaphysical and a focus on observable relations. Emblematic of this change was that Isaac Newton spent the early part of his life obsessed with the occult, filling notebooks with such machinations (Gleick, 2003), before turning his keen mind to observing nature. Auguste Comte is given credit for systematizing a philosophy of truth based on observation, known as *positivism*. Positivism, often carelessly associated with any empirical approach, is actually quite restricted and involves five principles (Hacking, 1983; Latour, 1999): (a) Verification is the idea that disputes can be settled in some way (i.e., the notion of falsification by observation), (b) observation—that which can be sensed—is the foundation of knowledge (with the exception of mathematical knowledge), (c) causality is simply the regularity of antecedents and consequences (i.e., co-occurrence), (d) explanations are used to organize observations but have no deeper underlying role (i.e., there is no deeper structure to be discovered), and (e) as a consequence, theory, as commonly discussed, has no role. Positivists rejected metaphysical constructs but by implication also rejected the notion of theory more generally. An orthodox positivist would reject the notion of psychological constructs and causality, thereby disapproving of most theories of psychotherapy. Behavior therapy has its roots in positivism (Fishman

& Franks, 1992), as it disallowed mentalistic constructs, focused on behavior (i.e., what can be observed), and sought functional relations rather than causality. On philosophical grounds, behaviorism would be considered more "scientific" because it emanates from the positivist tradition.

There is an interesting kink in the behaviorist adoption of positivism. If Treatment A, regardless of its nature, results in Outcome B, then its use and application are acceptable to behaviorists. So if hypnosis results in a reduction in smoking or eye movement desensitization and reprocessing reduces symptoms of posttraumatic stress disorder, these treatments are, to a radical behaviorist, behavior therapies. Behaviorists would, of course, reject the explanations provided by these theories because they involve mediating constructs that are not observable (Fishman & Franks, 1992), but the treatments themselves would be legitimate. Consequently, for the radical behaviorist, the introduction of cognitive components as theoretical constructs was problematic (Arnkoff & Glass, 1992; Fishman & Franks, 1992).

The positivist movement quickly was confronted with the thorny problems of language and meaning. The examination of language, meaning, and rational thought expanded positivism into what was known as *logical positivism,* which quickly left Comte's quaint notions behind and focused on logic, meaning, and the analysis of language. Logical positivism retained an emphasis on empiricism but incorporated notions of deductive logic and emphasized the role of language in science (i.e., logic was expressed through language structures). The idea of verification of propositions emanated from logical positivism (Hacking, 1983). It is not unusual to use the term *positivist* in a pejorative way to denote an obsession with observation, a lack of theory and thinking, and elimination of the mind from any social science.

The next philosophical school that is important for our purposes is *realism,* which allows for entities that are unobservable. The constructs posited by a theory, if the theory is correct, are as real as entities than can be observed (Hacking, 1983). Accordingly, the unconscious is as real, if psychodynamic theory is valid, as the facial tics that one can observe. Indeed, modern psychoanalytic theorists point to much evidence that supports the notion of the unconscious (Weinberger & Westen, 2001; Westen, 1998). Most psychotherapy theories assume a quasirealist perspective and entertain unobservable constructs, but from a realist perspective these actions depend on the validity of the theory. It is interesting to note that most of the heated debates at the origins of quantum theory were about philosophy of science—positivists versus realists—and whether mathematical solutions were legitimate even if they were devoid of observable evidence or even of entities that could be visualized (e.g., dimensions beyond four; Jones, 2008).

That an entity is unobservable does not detract from its usefulness, as illustrated by Louis Pasteur's discovery of germ theory:

> In 1864, Louis Pasteur "discovered" that microorganisms were the cause of fermentation without ever *observing* the organisms; the microorganisms revealed themselves through the results of clever experiments, and that evidence was more persuasive than earlier attempts to establish a germ theory of disease. That the organisms were not objectively observed or that the window on reality was not transparent does not distract from the evidence that Pasteur produced, the empirical enterprise that formed the basis of his investigations, or the subsequent interventions that followed (e.g., vaccinations, pasteurization, and sterilization). Pasteur's efforts were no more complex and no less controversial than investigations of the complexities of social interactions in many contexts, including, for example, Beebe, Knoblauch, Rustin, and Sorter's effort to understand *intersubjectivity* in infant and adult interactions, including therapy. (Wampold et al., 2007, p. 617)

A third school of philosophy that is germane to psychotherapy theory is *phenomenology*. Phenomenology, associated with the philosophers Kierkegaard, Husserl, Heidegger, and Sartre, is concerned with issues related to the structure of experience and consciousness, particularly from the subjective first-person perspective. The focus is not on the objective qualities of things, events, or interactions but on how they are perceived and interpreted by the individual. Phenomenology focuses on awareness of one's own experience, self-awareness, linguistic activity (including how language reciprocally influences experience and meaning making), and relationship with others (e.g., empathy). As mentioned in the previous chapter, phenomenology gave rise to humanistic and existential approaches to therapy.

The final thread in these philosophies is what is often called *constructivism* or *social constructivism,* sometimes classified as postmodern philosophy (Hacking, 1999; Latour, 1999). The critique of positivism and realism is that they either eschew theoretical entities entirely or posit some underlying truth, which can be investigated by experiment. Constructivism posits that humans construct meaning and that there is no objective truth about anything social (Latour, 1999). This movement has some antecedents in logical positivism but goes further to claim that social phenomena are primarily socially constructed realities. The predominant research approach in this area is qualitative research, such as grounded theory, which attempts to uncover the social constructions of the participants (Strauss & Corbin, 1998). As discussed in the previous chapter, multicultural counseling and psychotherapy, feminist therapy, and narrative therapy (Angus & McCloud, 2007) are closely allied to postmodern philosophy.

With this necessarily brief review, there are some important points to emphasize. In many ways, the schools of psychotherapy are derived from different philosophies of science: behavior therapy from positivism, psychoanalysis from realism (although Freud considered himself a positivist originally), humanistic and experiential therapy from phenomenology, and multicultural and narrative therapy from social constructivism. Because the philosophies differ, the ground rules for deciding the relative worth of these approaches differ—more technically, the theories are *incommensurable* (Hacking, 1983). Even the research methods used to investigate the theories differ; for example, Schneider (2008) claimed that phenomenological (qualitative) methods are necessary to investigate existential psychotherapies, whereas behavioral theories focus on objective measures of symptoms. Incommensurability implies that no amount of debate or research evidence will result in a determination of the relative worth of the various approaches. Theories of psychotherapy are descriptive and useful, but their validity is indeterminable, in an important sense.

As discussed previously, one way of settling the relative worth of various approaches is to simply examine empirically their effects—which treatment is more effective than another? There are several issues that render this strategy problematic. First, as discussed in the next chapter, there are few differences among treatments in terms of outcomes, so empirically it makes little sense to persist in comparing treatments intended to be therapeutic. Second, the effort to compare two treatments without regard to theoretical considerations is a positivist pursuit that provides little in the way of understanding, even if differences could be found. Third, despite efforts to separate them, methods and theory are always intertwined (Hacking, 1983). Comparative trials and ESTs are laden with behavioral and cognitive–behavioral aspects in terms of how outcomes are assessed (i.e., focus on symptoms) and how therapies are delivered (time limited and manualized). For example, experiential therapies are more focused on meaning and quality of life than on reduction of symptoms and are more difficult to manualize (Schneider, 2008).

SUMMARY

Psychotherapy theory is the road map that guides the therapist from Point A to Point B. Indeed, there can be no therapy without therapeutic actions, and the therapeutic actions emanate from theory. A cogent treatment is a fundamental element of psychotherapy. Choice of a theory involves multiple considerations on the part of the therapist and the client. Therapists, to be effective, need to have an allegiance to the theory—that is, they must believe that the application of the theory will result in benefits to the client. In addition, the client must believe in the explanation provided by the therapist. What is quite obvious to most observers is that master therapists practice widely divergent types of therapy and very often operate from an integration of theoretical orientations using interventions that are suitable and acceptable to the client. These therapists, although self-reflective, are passionate about the therapy approach they deliver.

Often therapists have an allegiance to a theoretical perspective without understanding fully the assumptions that come with the theory. The philosophy of science considerations render the theories incommensurable—

that is, there is no means to declare one theory superior to another. However, theory is absolutely necessary to guide practice.

Of course, theories have limits. As Wampold (2007) discussed, individuals presenting to a healer expect an explanation and treatment that are consistent with the system of healing. Patients in a medical context expect a biological explanation for their symptoms and a treatment consistent with that explanation (Wampold, Imel, et al., 2006). Accordingly, clients who present to a psychologist expect a psychological explanation, which then limits therapists to legitimate psychological approaches. Many "crazy" psychotherapies have been proposed over the years (Singer & Lalich, 1996), and although some practitioners might use them successfully, psychologists should provide a treatment that falls within what is considered the psychological field. Of course, the boundaries between legitimate and "crazy" are fuzzy, but there are a sufficient number of legitimate therapies from which to choose.

4

Research on the Effectiveness of Psychotherapy

Healing practices have been endemic to every human civilization since earliest times (A. K. Shapiro & Shapiro, 1997). Whether these practices actually healed or not is a matter of some interest. Some have claimed that many healing practices have actually been harmful. Acupuncture in ancient China, for example, may have killed many due to homologous serum jaundice, and George Washington may have died as a result of dehydrating treatments (e.g., bloodletting) administered for a respiratory condition (A. K. Shapiro & Shapiro, 1997; Wampold, 2001a). It is only recently that the research methods have been sufficient to investigate the effects of various interventions. The development of the randomized control group in the early 20th century allowed for the rigorous testing of the efficacy of various practices in agriculture, education, medicine, and psychology (Danziger, 1990; Gehan & Lemak, 1994; A. K. Shapiro & Shapiro, 1997). With regard to healing practices, only modern medicine and psychotherapy have been subjected to systematic controlled research to investigate the effectiveness of interventions (Wampold, 2007), and both practices have been shown to be effective, distinguishing them as the only practices scientifically shown to be effective. This chapter reviews the literature that shows that, indeed, psychotherapy is effective. The chapter then addresses the more difficult question of whether some approaches to psychotherapy are more effective than others. Finally, research on psychotherapy in the real world is discussed.

DOES PSYCHOTHERAPY WORK?

In the first decades of psychotherapy, the benefits of psychotherapy were established primarily by the presentation of successful cases by means of a certain treatment or technique. Psychoanalysis was supported by several perspicuous cases treated by Freud, including "Anna O.," "Dora," "Frau N.," "Little Hans," "Ratman," and "Wolfman." During the first half of the 20th century, research designs were developed to test the efficacy of various interventions and were applied most importantly in the area of medicine. The randomized double-blind placebo control group design became the gold standard for testing the efficacy of medicines (Gehan & Lemak, 1994; A. K. Shapiro & Shapiro, 1997); indeed, the design has been required for 3 decades by the U.S. Food and Drug Administration to approve drugs. It was not long after the development of this design that Rosenthal and Frank (1956) recommended it be used to investigate the effects of psychotherapy. Accordingly, there has been an increased use of randomized designs in psychotherapy research since then.

At the origins of the randomized design, the field's understanding of the effects of psychotherapy was, to say the least, ambiguous. On the one hand, Hans Eysenck, in a series of books and articles, made the claim that psychotherapy was not beneficial and was likely harmful (Eysenck, 1952, 1961, 1966; Wampold, 2001b). His claim was based on an examination of the rate of spontaneous remission of untreated patients, which was derived from two samples: "severe neurotics" receiving institutional custodial care and disability claims of "psychoneurotics." He then compared rates of recovery in psychotherapy studies with rates of spontaneous remission and found that recovery rates in psychotherapy groups were smaller than the rates of spontaneous remission. Indeed, he claimed, "There . . . appears to be an inverse correlation between recovery and psychotherapy; the more psychotherapy, the smaller the recovery rate" (Eysenck, 1952, p. 322). On the other hand, there were psychotherapy researchers who reviewed the literature on psychotherapy and reached exactly the opposite conclusion—that psychotherapy was indeed effective (Bergin, 1971; Luborsky, Singer, & Luborsky, 1975; Meltzoff & Kornreich, 1970). Needless to say, the controversy was not particularly beneficial to a field trying to establish its legitimacy as a healing practice.

Every controversy has it subtext. At the time of this controversy, the predominant approach to psychotherapy was either psychoanalytic or eclectic. Behavioral approaches to psychotherapy were emerging and struggling to be accepted as legitimate. Eysenck and others (e.g., Rachman, 1971) were making the claim that behavior therapy (as opposed to psychotherapy) was scientific and consequently superior to other approaches. In his later analyses, Eysenck (1961, 1966) made the claim that whereas psychotherapy (i.e., psychoanalysis and eclectic therapy) was ineffective or harmful, behavior therapy was remarkably effective. The historical context of Eysenck's claims have been discussed in some detail (M. L. Smith, Glass, & Miller, 1980; Wampold, 2001b).

A major event in the debate about the effects of psychotherapy was the development of meta-analysis as a means to objectively synthesize the results of many studies. In 1977, M. L. Smith and Glass collected all controlled research of psychotherapy, calculated an effect size for each treatment, and then averaged the effect sizes to estimate the degree to which the treatment group outcome exceeded the no-treatment group outcome. The intricacies of meta-analysis need not concern us here, but it is important to note that one of the lasting contributions of these earliest years of meta-analysis was that Glass (1976) developed an index of the effect size that was standardized—that is, it could be calculated regardless of the outcome measures used in the study. The measure of effect size indexed the degree to which the treatment group exceeded the control group in standard deviation units. In their comprehensive meta-analysis, M. L. Smith and Glass determined that the outcomes of those clients receiving psychotherapy were superior to the outcomes of those not receiving any treatment by .80 standard deviation units. As will become very clear later in this section, an effect size of .80 is remarkably large!

To the behaviorists, the M. L. Smith and Glass (1977) finding was disturbing because these authors found not only that psychotherapy was remarkably effective but also that behavior therapy was not substantially superior to other psychotherapies (a question considered in the next section). Consequently, the debate about the validity of the M. L. Smith and Glass meta-analysis became heated, with criticisms of meta-analysis as a method as well as of the authors' application of the method. One of the causes of the differences among the pre-meta-analytic reviews and the M. L. Smith and Glass meta-analysis was decisions about which studies to include and which to exclude. All of the earlier studies made an attempt to exclude poorly designed studies, but not surprisingly there were vociferous differences in opinion about the matter of quality; it is interesting to observe that the studies that supported the opposition in these debates were often excluded because of their (purported) poor quality (M. L. Smith et al., 1980). M. L. Smith and Glass attempted to address that issue by including all studies, regardless of quality, and then determining whether the quality of the study moderated the effect size. In this way, the question of whether better designed studies favored a particular treatment (say, behavioral) could be answered (better designed studies did not produce greater effects for behavioral treatments).

Nevertheless, M. L. Smith and Glass (1977) were criticized for omitting several important behavioral studies and for including studies that were poorly designed (Andrews & Harvey, 1981; Eysenck, 1978, 1984; Landman & Dawes, 1982). Moreover, there was criticism that many of the subjects in the studies meta-analyzed were mildly distressed and were not seeking treatment (e.g., psychology undergraduates). However, when these issues were addressed subsequently by critics of M. L. Smith and Glass in meta-analyses of good quality studies treating clients with significant psychological problems who were seeking treatment, the results were extraordinarily consistent with the M. L. Smith and Glass result of an effect size in the neighborhood of .80 (Andrews & Harvey, 1981; Dawes, 1994). Additional meta-analyses of psychotherapy outcomes have produced additional evidence that the effects of psychotherapy vis-à-vis no treatment are in the neighborhood of .80 (Wampold, 2001b).

We now turn to the question of whether an effect for psychotherapy of .80 is compelling. Is psychotherapy marginally, moderately, or extraordinarily effective? Of course, such evaluations are subjective, but recasting the effect size in various ways and comparing .80 with effects produced in other contexts provide a good sense of the size of this effect. An effect of .80 is equivalent to saying that 13% of the variability in outcomes is determined by whether one receives psychotherapy versus does not receive it (Wampold, 2001b); this is not particularly comforting on the face of it, because this means that 87% of the variability in mental health outcomes is not associated with whether a treatment is received or not! But conclusions should not be reached too quickly. An effect size of .80 also means that the average client receiving psychotherapy will be better off than 79% of those who do not receive treatment (M. L. Smith et al., 1980; Wampold, 2001b)—that is a common-sense interpretation that is particularly impressive. Most people in distress would be willing to receive a treatment with such odds.

Not only is psychotherapy effective, but it also appears that for many disorders, psychotherapy is as effective as pharmacological treatments for these disorders (Barlow, Gorman, Shear, & Woods, 2000; Hollon, Stewart, & Strunk, 2006; Imel, Malterer, McKay, & Wampold, 2008; Mitte, 2005; Mitte, Noack, Steil, & Hautzinger, 2005; Robinson, Berman, & Neimeyer, 1990). Moreover, it appears that when psychotherapy and medications are withdrawn (i.e., the psychotherapy is terminated or the course of medication is finished), the effects of psychotherapy are longer lasting (Hollon et al., 2006) in that at various times following the end of treatment, a greater number of clients who have been on medication relapse. It appears that psychotherapy provides clients with skills in coping with the world and their disorder. Moreover, clients who have received previous courses of medication become resistant to additional courses of medication, whereas they do not become resistant to additional courses of cognitive therapy (Leykin et al., 2007).

It is a safe conclusion that as a general class of healing practices, psychotherapy is remarkably effective. In clinical trials, psychotherapy results in benefits for patients that far exceed those for patients who do not get psychotherapy. Indeed, psychotherapy is more effective than many commonly used evidence-based medical practices, some of which have onerous side effects and are quite expensive (Wampold, 2007). As well, psychotherapy is as effective as medications for prevalent mental disorders, is longer lasting, and is less resistant to additional courses. This general finding leads us to the question of whether some types of psychotherapy are more effective than others.

ARE SOME PSYCHOTHERAPIES MORE EFFECTIVE THAN OTHERS?

The brief history of psychotherapy presented in chapter 2 showed that (a) many psychotherapies have been developed over the years; (b) advocates of these psychotherapies often make claims of superiority; (c) various schemes have been used to differentiate treatments based on the extent of the benefits experienced by clients; and (d) the debates about these issues have been contentious, to say the least. Indeed, as discussed previously, claims of superiority of a particular psychotherapy have characterized psychotherapy from the origins, with Freudians arguing with other Freudians, behaviorists criticizing psychoanalysis, and so forth. Indeed, Eysenck's (1952, 1961, 1966) claim of the ineffectiveness of psychotherapy was an attempt to show the superiority of behavior therapy, as based on the scientific principles of learning theory, to psychotherapy, as based on mentalistic and unscientific principles. It is not surprising that advocates of a treatment are convinced that their preferred treatment is as effective as or more effective than other treatments; people advocating any claim are generally convinced of its worth. Indeed, it is a good thing that those who develop a psychological treatment and those who practice it are enthusiastic supporters of the treatment, as discussed in chapter 3 of this volume.

Despite the flaws in many aspects of Eysenck's claims, his reviews were the first to use evidence from measures of outcomes of psychotherapy to address the question of the relative efficacy of various forms of psychotherapy. This section reviews the evidence, from the meta-analyses of M. L. Smith and colleagues (M. L. Smith & Glass, 1977; M. L. Smith et al., 1980) to the present, to show a result that may be surprising to some: When treatments that are intended to be therapeutic are compared, few differences among their outcomes are evident.

Psychotherapy in General

M. L. Smith and Glass's (1977) original meta-analysis addressed the issue of which type of psychotherapy was most effective. Given that this was the most rigorous and comprehensive review of psychotherapy outcomes to that time, their evidence provided the most scientifically valid answer to the question. The strategy used in this meta-analysis was to classify each of the nearly 800 effects obtained from psychotherapy outcome research into 1 of 10 classes of therapy: They found that about 10% of the variation in effects was due to the type of therapy, which provides some evidence that some types are more effective than other types. Adlerian, rational emotive, systematic desensitization, and behavior modification therapies were the most effective, with effect sizes in excess of .70. However, this analysis suffers from a number of problems, some of which M. L. Smith and Glass recognized and corrected.

A primary issue with M. L. Smith and Glass's (1977) attempt to compare classes of treatments was that the effects in each class were derived primarily from comparisons of the treatment with a no-treatment control. Thus, the studies in each class (say, systematic desensitization and Adlerian psychotherapy) were derived from different studies, and the different studies involved different disorders or problems, different dependent measures, different types of clients, different degrees of quality of the study, and so forth. M. L. Smith et al. (1980) sought to statistically control for these differences by coding characteristics of the studies. It turned out that controlling for the reactivity of the outcome measures, defined as the extent to which the measures "reveal[ed] or closely parallel[ed] the obvious goals or valued outcomes of the therapist or experimenter" (p. 66), by and large eliminated the differences among classes (viz., studies with behavioral treatments used more reactive measures and had larger effects). That is, the advantage for some classes of treatment was associated with studies that used more reactive measures. M. L. Smith and Glass's conclusion, after statistically controlling for reactivity of the measures and other variables, was that classes were generally equivalent. With regard to behavior and dynamic therapies, they noted that "In the original uncorrected data, the behavioral therapies did enjoy an advantage in the magnitude of effect because of more highly reactive measures. Once this advantage was corrected, reliable differences between the two classes [i.e., behavioral and dynamic] disappeared" (p. 105). M. L. Smith and Glass (1977) concluded, "Despite volumes devoted to the theoretical differences among different schools of psychotherapy, the results of research demonstrate negligible differences in the effects produced by different therapy types" (p. 760). It was this finding—that behavioral treatments were not clearly more effective than other treatments—rather than the finding that psychotherapy was effective that instigated much of the criticism of the M. L. Smith and Glass meta-analyses (Eysenck, 1978; Rachman & Wilson, 1980; Wilson, 1982; Wilson & Rachman, 1983).

As M. L. Smith and Glass (1977) recognized, the best way to control for most confounding variables was to aggregate only those studies that directly compared two treatments, as the measures used, quality of the design, types of clients, disorder treated, and so forth would be equivalent for each comparison. M. L. Smith and Glass attempted to do this. Although the results were equivalent to their general conclusions, there were a number of problems with their analysis, the least of which was that there were few studies that compared treatments fairly (Wampold, 2001b).

D. A. Shapiro and Shapiro (1982a, 1982b) sought to address the confound problem by examining studies that directly compared two treatments, and they included the behavioral studies that M. L. Smith and Glass were criticized for omitting (Rachman & Wilson, 1980). All of the studies analyzed also contained a no-treatment control, and they found an overall effect size that was consistent with the .80 found by M. L. Smith and Glass (Wampold, 2001b). The results of this meta-analysis are complex because the direct comparisons between classes of treatments were few for some classes (e.g., no studies compared dynamic therapy to systematic desensitization, whereas 24 studies compared systematic desensitization to relaxation). Nevertheless, among classes of treatments, excluding treatments that had minimal aspects of a "real" psychotherapy, only two comparisons were significant out of 14 comparisons: Cognitive therapy was superior to systematic desensitization, and mixed therapies were superior to systematic desensitization. It appears that the superiority of cognitive therapy to systematic desensitization was an anomaly, because other meta-analyses have found that there were no differences among these two classes and that there were large differences for researcher allegiances (Berman, Miller, & Massman, 1985).

One of the problems with the D. A. Shapiro and Shapiro (1982a, 1982b) meta-analysis was the classification of treatment into categories. The first issue is that it is often difficult to classify treatments into categories, and the agreement about this process is suspect. The second issue is that the classification strategy prevents tests of the treatments within classes, even though such treatments might be quite different (e.g., Freudian psychoanalysis and short-term focused dynamic therapy would be classified most likely as "dynamic therapies"). The third issue is that pairwise comparisons among classes of therapies yield a large number of statistical tests (actually, if there are k classes of treatments, then there are $k(k-1)/2$ comparisons, which grows large quickly—e.g., six classes of treatments yield 15 statistical comparisons).

Wampold and colleagues (1997) devised a meta-analytic procedure that avoided the problems of classifying treatments, as well as some others. They collected all comparisons of treatments intended to be therapeutic. The inclusion of treatments that were intended to be therapeutic was invoked to eliminate control group treatments that were designed to rule out particular common factors, such as a relationship with an empathic healer. These treatments, often called *psychological placebos, alternative treatments, common factor controls,* or *supportive counseling,* have no reasonable rationale that can be communicated to clients; therapists are proscribed from discussing certain topics; and the control treatment contains no ingredients that are based on psychological principles (see Wampold et al., 1997). Including only treatments intended to be therapeutic eliminated the problems that occurred previously (D. A. Shapiro & Shapiro, 1982a, 1982b) when several classes of psychotherapies may have contained treatments that were clearly not "real" psychotherapies, which complicated interpretations of D. A. Shapiro and Shapiro's (1982a, 1982b) "mixed" and "minimal" classifications. It really doesn't make much sense to make claims about the efficacy of psychotherapy when treatments are included that would not qualify as psychotherapy given the usual definition, as presented in chapter 1.

Following the lead of the D. A. Shapiro and Shapiro (1982b) and the advice of Shadish and Sweeney (1991), Wampold et al. (1997) analyzed only studies that directly compared two or more psychotherapies intended to be therapeutic. They collected all such comparative studies from 1970 to 1995 published in the six premier journals that published psychotherapy outcome research, which yielded 277 direct comparisons. The analyses of these direct comparisons created some issues for the analysis: Wampold et al.'s primary solution was to examine the distribution of the effects rather than their mean. If the dodo bird conjecture is true (see chapter 2, this volume) and all psychotherapies intended to be therapeutic are equally effective, occasionally, due to sampling, a study will appear that demonstrates a relatively large difference between the two treatments, but on the whole most studies will reveal differences close to zero.

Wampold et al. (1997) found that when modeled in this way, most comparisons between treatments yielded effects very close to zero, and the few larger effects were not unexpected, given the role of random sampling. That is to say, the obtained distribution of effects from these comparisons provided no evidence to suggest that some treatments were more effective than others (in more technical language, the effects were homogenously distributed around zero).

For some, the various meta-analyses of different types of psychotherapy provided evidence that the dodo was correct—"all have won, and all must have prizes"—as Rosenzweig (1936) suggested. Of course, to those who staunchly believed that some treatments were more effective than others (e.g., advocates of empirically supported treatments [ESTs]), this conclusion was uncomfortable. In response to the question about whether

ESTs are more effective than non-ESTs, Ollendick and King (2006) stated, "At some level, the answer to this question is patently obvious and resoundingly in the affirmative" (p. 308). The divergence of the conclusions from the evidence on the relative efficacy of different psychotherapies is well illustrated by a chapter that presented the pro and con arguments for the superiority of ESTs (Wampold, Ollendick, & King, 2006). Because this issue is far from settled, for those beginning to learn various approaches to psychotherapy, it seems unwarranted at this point to limit this endeavor to the ESTs.

To be sure, there was a very valid criticism of the meta-analyses of M. L. Smith and Glass (1977; M. L. Smith et al., 1980), D. A. Shapiro and Shapiro (1982b), and Wampold et al. (1997). In each of these meta-analyses, studies were aggregated without regard to the disorder being treated, which

> is akin to asking whether insulin or an antibiotic is better, without knowing the condition for which these treatments are to be given. . . . Alternatively, researchers should begin with a problem and ask how treatments compare in their effectiveness for that problem. (DeRubeis, Brotman, & Gibbons, 2005, p. 175)

This sentiment was echoed by others (Crits-Christoph, 1997) and is not a criticism easily dismissed; the next section addresses this criticism.

For Specific Disorders

Space does not allow an examination of the literature for all diagnoses, so here the review is constrained to the most prevalent mental disorders, depression and anxiety disorders, as well as alcohol use disorders, personality disorders, and childhood disorders.

Depression

By 1998, many treatments were designated as ESTs for depression, including behavior therapy, cognitive therapy, interpersonal therapy, brief dynamic therapy, reminiscence therapy (for geriatric populations), self-control therapy, and social problem-solving therapy (Chambless et al., 1998). If the EST list were updated today, many additional treatments would need to be added, including process experiential therapy (Ollendick & King, 2006), which has been shown to be equally effective as cognitive–behavioral therapy (CBT; J. C. Watson, Gordon, Stermac, Kalogerakos, & Steckley, 2003), the most validated psychotherapy for any disorder. Thus, it appears that a variety of treatments, based on a variety of theories, have been shown to be effective for the treatment of depression.

Meta-analyses of clinical trials of depression have consistently verified, with some qualifications, that all treatments of depression are equally effective. An early meta-analysis (Robinson et al., 1990) classified treatments into four categories: cognitive, behavioral, cognitive–behavioral, and verbal. The latter contained dynamic, humanistic, and experiential treatments. Generally, they found that behavioral, cognitive–behavioral, and cognitive treatments were superior to general verbal therapies and that CBT was superior to behavioral therapy. Two critical issues—ones that were discussed in the previous section—complicate interpretation of the results. First, likely many of the verbal therapies in these comparisons were not treatments that were really intended to be therapeutic—that is, some of the verbal therapies were in actuality control groups meant to control for common factors such as meeting with an empathic therapist. As has been discussed, this type of treatment typically has no cogent rationale for the treatment and few actions that practicing psychotherapists would consider to be therapeutic. A later meta-analysis found that cognitive therapy for depression was superior to "other" therapies, which were noncognitive, nonbehavioral treatments (Gloaguen, Cottraux, Cucherat, & Blackburn, 1998). However, many of the "other" treatments were not intended to be therapeutic; when these treatments were omitted, cognitive therapy was not superior to "other" treatments intended to be therapeutic (Wampold, Minami, Baskin, & Tierney, 2002).

The second, and not unrelated, issue is that of researcher allegiance. It is well documented that the allegiance of the researcher exerts quite large and robust effects on the results of studies; that is, studies conducted by an advocate of a particular treatment consistently find effects for that particular treatment (Berman et al., 1985; Luborsky et al., 1999; Wampold, 2001b). The explanation for allegiance effects is somewhat ambiguous, leaving unanswered the question, How does the allegiance of the researcher translate into larger effects for the favored treatment? There are several possibilities, including translation of researcher allegiance to therapist allegiance (e.g., the therapists in the study know which is the preferred treatment, as would be the case when the researcher trains and supervises the therapists), the study design favors one treatment (e.g., the preferred treatment has a greater dose of therapy), or the comparison treatment is poorly constructed (e.g., the therapists in the comparison are proscribed from commonly used therapeutic actions; Luborsky et al., 1999; Wampold, 2001b). The latter explanation results in the inclusion of treatments not intended to be therapeutic, which often populate classes of treatments labeled as "verbal therapies" or "other therapies." When Robinson et al. (1990) took into account the allegiance of the researcher, all of the differences among the various categories were not significantly different from zero. That is to say, allegiance accounted for all of the differences among the classes of treatments of depression.

Subsequent meta-analyses of treatments of depression have generally confirmed that there are no differences among such treatments (e.g., Cuijpers, van Straten, Andersson, & van Oppen, 2008; Wampold, Minami, et al., 2002). However, some studies have shown the superiority of two treatments (interpersonal therapy and behavioral activation) to CBT for severe depression (Dimidjian et al., 2006; Elkin et al., 1995), although the sizes of the effects were not large.

Many have argued that it is not surprising that treatments for depression are generally equivalent because acute depression is responsive to interventions. Anxiety disorders, however, are often used to make claims about the superiority of some treatments over others.

Anxiety Disorders

The progression of meta-analyses, in which various problems in early ones were addressed in later ones, that was seen for depression is not the same for anxiety disorders, generally. However, there is sufficient evidence to draw some tentative conclusions. As will be shown, there is insufficient evidence to conclude that any particular treatment for any anxiety disorder is clearly superior to any other treatment, although there are clearly some treatments that have sufficient evidence to conclude that they are effective treatments.

Wampold (2001b) reviewed all of the meta-analyses for the treatment of anxiety disorders and found little evidence for the superiority of any treatment. However, for most anxiety disorders, there were an insufficient number of direct comparisons among treatments intended to be therapeutic to be conclusive. This section briefly reviews the research since that time.

There are more clinical trials and more treatments studied in the area of posttraumatic stress disorder (PTSD) than for any other anxiety disorder. Over the years, many treatments have been developed and tested for PTSD, including CBT (Foa et al., 2005; Foa, Rothbaum, Riggs, & Murdock, 1991), eye-movement desensitization and reprocessing (EMDR; Rothbaum, Astin, & Marsteller, 2005; F. Shapiro, 1989); cognitive therapy without exposure (Tarrier et al., 1999), hypnotherapy (Brom, Kleber, & Defares, 1989); psychodynamic therapy (Brom et al., 1989); and present-centered therapy (McDonagh et al., 2005). Clearly, the theoretical rationales of these treatments vary widely, including conditioning, cognitive restructuring, psychodynamics, and neuropsychology. Some of the treatments were intentionally designed to exclude exposure and/or cognitive restructuring (e.g., McDonagh et al., 2005; Tarrier et al., 1999), some are what several researchers have characterized as scientifically unjustified (e.g., EMDR; Herbert et al., 2000), and some are based on "old-fashioned" mentalistic constructs (e.g., hypnotherapy and dynamic therapies). Because PTSD is a disorder that is attributable to a discrete event or series of events, it would seem that treatments based on scientific psychological explanations would be developed and that these treatments would be more effective than other treatments. Nevertheless, recently Benish, Imel, and Wampold (2008) used the meta-analytic methods of Wampold et al. (1997) to aggregate effects from all studies that directly compared two or more treatments intended to be therapeutic for PTSD. They found, for PTSD symptom measures and for all measures, little evidence that treatment differences existed; if they did, the effects were very small. It appears that the current evidence for the treatment of PTSD does not support the conclusion that one particular treatment is superior to any other; given the variety of treatments studied, a conclusion could be made that all treatments for PTSD that have a cogent theoretical rationale, delivered by competent therapists who believe in the treatment to clients who seek out the treatment, are equally effective.

An interesting pattern develops in the treatment of various disorders that is illustrated by the treatment of panic disorder. Panic disorder is a fairly circumscribed disorder in that the symptoms are easily recognizable, although panic disorder and other anxiety disorders (e.g., not surprisingly, agoraphobia) frequently co-occur. The first treatments focused on the symptoms of panic disorder were cognitive–behavioral and behavioral (primarily relaxation therapy [RT]), and they were found to be quite effective in comparison with no-treatment controls or treatments that attempted to control for common factors (see, e.g., Barlow, Craske, Cerny, & Klosko, 1989). Most of the comparisons for treatments of panic disorder compared either behavioral with cognitive–behavioral treatments or one of these with pharmacological treatments. One meta-analysis found that the cognitive components of CBT did not add to the efficacy of behavioral treatments for panic but that the cognitive components did seem to improve symptoms of depression (Mitte, 2005). But another meta-analysis, by Siev and Chambless (2007), found that CBT was superior to RT, a behavioral treatment, for the treatment of panic without severe agoraphobia on measures of panic symptoms but not on other measures (e.g., anxiety and depression); these results, however, were based a small number of comparisons (four or five, depending on the analysis). The hegemony of cognitive and behavioral treatments for panic may have much to do with the early development and testing of these treatments. The testing of treatments less easily manualized than cognitive and behavioral treatments has lagged behind. Nevertheless, recently a well-controlled study of psychoanalytic psychotherapy for panic disorder showed that this treatment is a viable treatment as well (Milrod et al., 2007). Some would claim that as additional treatments for panic are developed and tested, they will be found to be as effective as the cognitive and cognitive–behavioral treatments (Wampold, 2001b).

Other comparisons of approaches to treating anxiety disorders have shown similar results. A study directly comparing a behavioral treatment (response prevention/exposure) and CBT for obsessive–compulsive disorder showed results not consistently favoring one treatment or another (Cottraux et al., 2001; Emmelkamp, Visser, & Hoekstra, 1988; Simons, Schneider, & Herpertz-Dahlmann, 2006; Van Oppen, de Haan, Van Balkom, & Spinhoven, 1995; Whittal, Thordarson, & McLean, 2005), and a recent meta-analysis comparing similar treatments found that the effect sizes produced were not significantly different (Rosa-Alcázar, Sánchez-Meca, Gómez-Conesa, & Marín-Martínez, 2008). Comparisons of treatments of generalized anxiety disorder (Siev & Chambless, 2007) and social anxieties (Acarturk, Cuijpers, van Straten, & de Graaf, 2009) show similar results.

In general, there is no evidence that any particular treatment for any particular anxiety disorder is reliably more effective than any other, with the possible exception that CBT is more effective than RT for panic. However, this conclusion is tempered by the fact that for most anxiety disorders, only some variants of behavioral and cognitive–behavioral treatments have been tested. However, when other viable treatments for anxiety disorders are developed and tested, they seem to fare as well as the cognitive and behavioral treatments.

Substance Use Disorders

There is a wide range of treatments for substance use disorders, including CBT, motivational interviewing, 12-step programs, and social skills training, among others. Well-designed trials have found few differences among various treatments (Project Match Research Group, 1997). Again, the most recent meta-analysis to examine direct comparisons of treatments for alcohol use disorders found no differences among this wide array of treatments in either alcohol use measures or abstinence measures (Imel, Wampold, Miller, & Fleming, 2008), a result not inconsistent with previous meta-analyses in this area.

Personality Disorders

The most widely known systematic treatment for a personality disorder is dialectical behavior therapy (DBT) for borderline personality disorder, developed by Linehan (1993). DBT contains cognitive–behavioral components as well as mindfulness techniques to regulate emotion, client support, and increasing therapist self-efficacy and skills to treat clients with borderline personality features. DBT has been shown to be effective relative to various control conditions, including treatment as usual (TAU) by expert community therapists (Linehan et al., 2006).

Recently, however, psychodynamic theorists have developed several treatments for personality disorders (Clarkin, Levy, Lenzenweger, & Kernberg, 2007). DBT was compared with transference-focused psychotherapy, a psychodynamic therapy, and it was found that both of these structured treatments were effective across multiple outcome domains but that the transference-focused psychotherapy was superior to DBT in terms of impulsivity, anger, irritability, and aggressiveness outcomes (Clarkin et al., 2007). Although there are relatively few studies of treatment for personality disorders, particularly compared with mood disorders, Leichsenring and Leibing (2003) conducted a meta-analysis of psychodynamic treatments and CBT for personality disorders and found that generally the effects for psychodynamic therapy were as large as or larger than the effects for CBT. However, many of the studies in this meta-analysis were not well controlled, and few studies directly compared CBT and psychodynamic therapies. In conclusion, it does not appear that any one treatment for personality disorders is more effective than another, although it does appear that psychodynamic treatments hold their own against, and may even be superior to, CBT.

Childhood Disorders

A number of meta-analyses have been conducted on psychotherapies for children. It is difficult to compare effects obtained for treatment of children with effects for adults because the manner in which the effect sizes are calculated differs, based in part on the design of the studies and advances in statistical methods over the years. Nevertheless, it appears that psychotherapy is effective with children, although perhaps not as effective as it is with adults (Weisz, McCarty, & Valeri, 2006; Weisz, Weiss, Han, Granger, & Morton, 1995). There is some debate about whether cognitive and behavioral treatments are more effective than other treatments for children. In 1995, Weisz et al. conducted a meta-analysis and concluded that behavioral treatments were superior to nonbehavioral treatments for children. It was claimed that this superiority may be artifactual, but Weiss and Weisz (1995) examined one such artifact, quality of the studies, and found that this was not a threat to the superiority of behavioral treatments. A later meta-analysis found that CBT was not superior to noncognitive treatments for children with depression (Weisz, McCarty, et al., 2006). The lack of direct comparisons in these meta-analyses poses a threat to the validity of the conclusions, however, a problem that has been addressed in some recent meta-analyses.

Spielmans, Pasek, and McFall (2007) aggregated the effects for direct comparisons of CBT and other treatments for children with depression and anxiety. They found that CBT was superior to treatments not intended to be therapeutic but was not superior to other treatments when those treatments were intended to be therapeutic for the disorder. Miller, Wampold, and Varhely (2008) analyzed all studies between 1980 and 2005 that directly compared two treatments intended to be therapeutic for children with depression, anxiety, conduct disorder, and attention-deficit/hyperactivity disorder. They found that the effects were not homogenously distributed around zero, in contrast to Wampold et al. (1997), indicating that perhaps some treatments were more effective than others. The differences among treatments were completely explained by the allegiance of the researcher, however: Studies produced effects in favor of one treatment when the researcher had an allegiance to that treatment. For example, if the researcher of the treatment for which there was an allegiance trained and supervised the therapists for both treatments, there tended to be an effect for that preferred treatment. In any event, the effect for differences detected by Miller et al. (2008) was, at most, very small and similar to that of adults. As was the case for adults, it does not appear that any one approach to treating children is more effective than others.

Relative Efficacy Conclusions

It appears that in general and for specific disorders, no treatment has been consistently shown to be superior to any other treatment intended to be therapeutic. There are some limitations to this conclusion, however. There have been some demonstrations, albeit weak, that some treatments are superior. For example, Siev and Chambless (2007) found that CBT was superior to relaxation for panic disorder with agoraphobia on some outcome domains in a meta-analysis of five studies. CBT for severe depression seems to be less effective than some alternatives (viz., behavioral activation and interpersonal therapy). Psychodynamic treatment seems to be more effective than a CBT variant for borderline personality disorder, at least in one trial, and for personality disorders in general in a meta-analysis. However, when contrasted with the many studies and many meta-analyses that have shown no differences among treatments, it is difficult to make recommendations on the basis of the small differences that have been found.

PSYCHOTHERAPY IN THE REAL WORLD

Most of the evidence about psychotherapy reviewed in this chapter has been derived from clinical trials. Because of the nature of the delivery of mental health services in naturalistic settings, including the confidential nature of the service and the relative autonomy afforded professionals, very little is known about services in practice settings. This is beginning to change as more systems of care begin to assess outcomes, and various national surveys have been conducted to assess treatment of mental disorders. The major findings of this service research are briefly summarized in this section.

The most important question is whether psychotherapy delivered in naturalistic settings is effective. Although reviews of controlled research indicate that psychotherapy is remarkably effective, there is no guarantee that it works as well when delivered in real-world practice settings. There have been three strategies for addressing this issue. The first strategy is to assess the degree to which treatments delivered in controlled research resemble treatments that would be delivered in practice; this is sometimes referred to as *clinical representativeness*. In general, it has been found that the degree to which a treatment is representative of clinic settings is unrelated to the effect size produced; that is, those treatments that resemble treatments in practice are no less effective than those delivered in highly controlled laboratory settings (Shadish et al., 1997; Shadish, Navarro, & Matt, 2000).

The second strategy is to implement a treatment in a field setting and compare outcomes with treatment as usual (sometimes called *usual care* or *standard care*). Typically, the treatment imported to the field setting is an EST or evidence-based treatment (EBT) developed and tested in more controlled conditions. The hypothesis of TAU studies is that the quality of service would be improved by transporting ESTs to field settings (Minami & Wampold, 2008). For a number of disorders for both children and adults, these studies have found that ESTs or EBTs delivered in field settings produce better outcomes than TAUs (Addis et al., 2004; Linehan et al., 2006; Weisz, Jensen-Doss, & Hawley, 2006). However, there are a number of caveats. Often, the therapists in the EST or EBT receive extra supervision and training, often by the author who also developed the EST or EBT. In other cases, the TAU is not a psychotherapy (e.g., is a support group) and involves much less contact with the client. In any event, the differences between the EBT or EBT and the TAU are quite small and, in the better controlled studies, not significantly different (Minami & Wampold, 2008).

The third strategy to assess outcomes in clinical settings is known as *benchmarking*. The idea of benchmarking is to calculate the effect of psychotherapy in clinical trials (say, the effect from pretherapy to posttherapy) and then calculate the same effect in a naturalistic setting. In an early benchmarking study, Weersing and Weisz (2002) calculated the benchmark via meta-analytic methods and found that TAU for 67 children produced effects that were closer to effects of no-treatment controls than to effects of treatments in clinical trials. Unfortunately, benchmarking requires large samples to provide reliable estimates, and the methods to compare effects are complex. Recently, Minami and colleagues developed benchmarking strategies (Minami, Serlin, Wampold, Kircher, & Brown, 2008) and meta-analytically created benchmarks for the treatment of depression in adults (Minami, Wampold, Serlin, Kircher, & Brown, 2007). Using data from a managed care environment where outcomes were assessed involving several thousand clients who had a diagnosis of depression, the results obtained in practice met or exceeded the benchmarks established in clinical trials (Minami, Wampold, et al., 2008).

It appears that treatment in practice is effective, if not as effective as treatments delivered in clinical trials. There is some evidence that TAU might be inferior to ESTs or EBTs transported to practice settings, but the differences are small and the extra training and supervision and increased intensity of treatment render the comparisons difficult to interpret. The latter result, though, raises the possibility that some treatments in practice are more effective than others—is the dodo bird conclusion applicable to field settings? Again, evidence from field settings is difficult to obtain, but efforts have been made to address this question with psychotherapy provided in the context of primary care in the National Health Service in the United Kingdom, where outcomes are routinely assessed. Providers indicated whether they were delivering CBT, person-centered therapy, or psychodynamic therapy. In two studies with large samples, the outcomes produced by providers were generally equivalent across the three treatments (Stiles, Barkham, Mellor-Clark, & Connell, 2008; Stiles, Barkham, Twigg, Mellor-Clark, & Cooper, 2006). This finding suggests that the general equivalence of treatments found in clinical trials is also true in practice.

Given that it appears that the type of therapy provided does not affect outcomes, it is worth knowing what approaches therapists use. Every 10 years, Norcross and colleagues survey members of Division 29 (Psychotherapy) of the American Psychological Association to determine, in part, what types of therapy are being provided. In the most recent survey (Norcross, Hedges, & Castle, 2002), more than one third of the psychologists indicated that their practice was eclectic or integrative, followed by psychodynamic or psychoanalytic (29%), behavioral or cognitive (19%; about double what it was in 1981), and some form of humanistic (person-centered, Rogerian, existential, gestalt, or other humanistic; 6%, down from 14% in 1981). It appears that cognitive and behavior approaches are increasing in popularity and that humanistic approaches are declining.

There is a sense in many quarters that the dose of therapy needs to be limited because clients will tend to use more psychotherapy than is necessary to treat the disorder. The evidence does not support this assumption, however. In the benchmarking study discussed above (Minami, Wampold, et al., 2008), the clients, whose service was not limited, used on average 9 sessions to meet the depression benchmarks, whereas the average number of sessions in clinical trials used to create the benchmarks was 16 (Minami, Wampold, et al., 2008). That is to say, not only is psychotherapy delivered in practice effective; it is also efficient! Stiles, Barkham, Connell, and Mellor-Clark (2008) found that clients and therapists appropriately adjusted the length of therapy to fit the needs of the clients and that when clients made sufficient improvement, they terminated therapy (see also Baldwin, Berkeljon, Atkins, Olsen, & Nielsen, 2009).

The effectiveness of psychotherapy in the real world is well documented, but the truth is that any strategy to improve outcomes would be immensely valuable as long as some positive change occurs. But what of cases where there is no change or, worse, cases that deteriorate? By some accounts, 5% to 10% of clients in therapy deteriorate (Bergin, 1971; Hansen, Lambert, & Forman, 2002). In the past decade, there has been an increased emphasis on measuring outcomes in routine practice and using this information to improve outcomes (Lambert, Hansen, & Finch, 2001; Miller, Duncan, & Hubble, 2005). Of particular interest is the research on providing feedback to therapists about the outcomes achieved by their clients. In a series of studies, Lambert and colleagues (Harmon et al., 2007; Lambert, Harmon, Slade, Whipple, & Hawkins, 2005; Lambert, Whipple, et al., 2001; Lambert et al., 2002; Whipple et al., 2003) investigated the effects of informing therapists whether a particular client is making expected progress (i.e, improving at a rate expected for clients of a given level of severity), is not making expected progress but is improving, or is deteriorating. This research has shown that the clients of therapists who received this simple feedback attained better outcomes at the end of treatment than clients of therapists who did not receive feedback. The effect was particularly large for clients who were deteriorating.

CONCLUSION

Although historically there have been debates about the effects of psychotherapy, the research clearly demonstrates that psychotherapy is a
remarkably effective treatment—more effective than many medical
practices and as effective as medications for most mental disorders.
Nevertheless, it appears, with some possible exceptions, that treatments
intended to be therapeutic are generally equally effective, across disorders as well as for specific disorders. In general, no one theory is more
effective than any other. It also appears that psychotherapy delivered in
practice settings is as effective or nearly as effective as psychotherapy
provided in clinical trials.

5

How Does Psychotherapy Work?

Historically, there has been a tension between those who believe that particular treatments for various disorders are effective because of the specific ingredients of the treatments and those who believe that therapeutic ingredients common to all (or most) treatments are responsible for the benefits of psychotherapy. So, in some ways, what makes psychotherapy works depends on whom you ask. In this chapter, the evidence for specific ingredients is presented, followed by the evidence for common factors.

EVIDENCE FOR SPECIFIC INGREDIENTS

In medicine, specificity is established in two ways. First, a medicine (or a procedure) is compared to a placebo in a double-blind randomized control group design, which controls for the psychological factors, such as hope, expectancy, and relationship with a healer. If the medication is found to be superior to the placebo, then there is evidence that the specific ingredients of the medication are responsible for the benefits because the only difference between the active medication and placebo conditions is the specific ingredient purported to be remedial for the medical condition. The second way that specificity is established in medicine is to establish a system-specific sequence (Wampold, 2007). According to Wampold (2007), this is accomplished in the following way:

> (a) a biological explanation for the illness, based on scientific research, is established; (b) a treatment is designed or a substance is hypothesized to remediate the biological deficit; (c) administration of the substance demonstrably alters the biology of the patient in the expected way, and other substances do not; and (d) the change in the biology remediates the illness (a cure or management of chronic illness). (p. 867)

An example of the system-specific sequence involves the treatment of peptic ulcers. Peptic ulcers are hypothesized to be caused by the presence of a significant population of the bacterium *Helicobacter pylori,* the treatment consists (in part) of the administration of an antibiotic that reduces the population of bacteria, administration of the treatment indeed does reduce the population of bacteria, and the client subsequently improves (symptoms disappear and tests reveal that the ulcer has healed).

Psychotherapy researchers have used various experimental designs similar to the randomized placebo design and various other types of design to establish the system-specific sequence in an attempt to establish specificity in psychotherapy. In many ways, establishing specificity is more difficult in psychotherapy than it is in medicine because of inherent difficulties in measuring processes and outcomes in psychological systems, because double blinding is not possible in psychotherapy trials, and because the psychological deficits in various mental disorders are ambiguous. Nevertheless, the next section presents a brief review of the evidence for specificity, organized by type of design.

Component Designs

Component designs attempt to isolate the effects of particular ingredients by either removing a critical ingredient (often called a *dismantling design*), which should attenuate the benefits of the treatment, or by adding an ingredient (often called *additive designs*), which is hypothesized to increase the potency of the treatment (Borkovec, 1990). Next, two examples of component designs illustrate the logic and provide prototypical results.

Cognitive–behavioral therapy (CBT) for depression, the most studied and validated psychotherapy without a doubt, is composed of three primary components: behavioral activation, acquisition of skills to interrupt and change automatic thoughts, and modification of core schemata. Jacobson et al. (1996), in an attempt to establish the importance of the cognitive components, randomly assigned 150 clients with depression to one of three conditions: behavioral activation (BA); behavioral activation plus ingredients purported to change automatic thoughts (AT); and the full package (CBT), which also addresses the core cognitive schemata. At the end of treatment and at 6-month follow-up, CBT was not was not more effective than either of the two components. Moreover, BA and AT changed automatic thoughts and dysfunctional attributional styles as much as CBT. These results suggest that the cognitive components of CBT are not specific for the treatment of depression; that is, the work on automatic thoughts and dysfunctional core attributions is not critical to the success of CBT for depression.

Resick et al. (2008) used a similar strategy to dismantle cognitive processing therapy (CPT) for posttraumatic stress disorder (PTSD) for female victims of interpersonal violence. The full CPT was compared with treatments that were composed of one of the two main components of CPT: written accounts of the traumatic violence (WA) and cognitive therapy without the written accounts (CT). Clients in all three conditions improved substantially on measures of PTSD symptoms and depression. The full treatment (i.e., CPT) was not significantly better than either of the two components, although CT was slightly superior to WA on PTSD measures. Similar to Jacobson et al. (1996), the full treatment was not superior to treatments containing some of the components, suggesting that the components were not specific for treating PTSD.

In 2001, Ahn and Wampold meta-analyzed all studies that used component designs to assess the specific ingredients. They were able to locate 27 studies that either removed a critical component or added a component to determine whether the full treatment package was superior to a treatment with fewer (or no) critical components. The effect for the difference between the treatment with and without the critical components was not significantly different from zero, indicating that across all of these studies, there was not consistently a demonstration that the hypothesized critical ingredients were critical to the success of the treatment.

In a meta-analysis of social anxiety, Acarturk, Cuijpers, van Straten, and de Graaf (2009) examined various treatments that contained various hypothesized ingredients. Although these were not component studies, they addressed the same issue. In this meta-analysis, treatments without exposure were not significantly different from those with exposure, treatments without relaxation were not significantly different from those with relaxation, and those with social skills training were not significantly different from those without social skills training.

Shortly after the development of the placebo control group design in medicine, Rosenthal and Frank (1956) suggested it be used in psychotherapy research to establish the specificity of psychological treatments. Unfortunately, use of the placebo control group design in psychotherapy is problematic in ways that demonstrate the differences between psychotherapy and medicine (Baskin, Tierney, Minami, & Wampold, 2003; Critelli & Neumann, 1984; Grünbaum, 1981; A. K. Shapiro & Morris, 1978; Shepherd, 1993; Wampold, 1997, 2001a, 2001b). The basic design of a psychological placebo has involved the creation of a treatment without any specific ingredients—that is, an inert psychological process. These placebo-type treatments are often called *supportive counseling, alternative treatments,* or *common factor controls.* The treatments have no psychological basis and often consist of empathic responding or reflective listening but no focus on particular problems, coping skills, and so forth (i.e., there is no cogent rationale for the treatment). Sometimes, to control for certain specific ingredients, therapists are proscribed from responding in certain common ways. For example, to control for exposure in the treatment of PTSD, the placebo-type controls may require that the therapist not discuss the traumatic event, as this would be a form of covert or imaginal exposure (e.g., thinking about the event in a safe and comfortable environment; see, e.g., Foa, Rothbaum, Riggs, & Murdock, 1991).

There are three primary problems with placebo groups in psychotherapy research. First is the problem of distinguishability. In medicine, the pill placebo and the active pill are indistinguishable, whereas in psychotherapy they are quite different. That is, the active treatment and the placebo differ on many dimensions besides simply inclusion of the active ingredient, including the credibility of the treatment to the clients and the expectations that might be created by the actions. The best-designed placebos attempt to create a credible rationale for the treatment (Borkovec & Costello, 1993). But placebos are often quite deficient, delivering a smaller dose of therapy or using less skilled therapists (Baskin et al., 2003).

A second related problem is that placebo psychotherapy studies cannot be blinded. Clients may not know much about the various treatments in a study, but they certainly are aware of the ingredients of each condition because they are receiving them. More problematic, however, is that the therapists in the study are not blinded; typically, they know they are providing either an experimental, novel, and innovative treatment or a therapy without any active ingredients.

The third problem is that the placebo control groups do not contain all of the common factors, particularly a cogent rationale and a treatment, two of the most critical common factors in many models, as was discussed in previous chapters (Frank & Frank, 1991; Garfield, 1992; Imel & Wampold, 2008; Torrey, 1972; Wampold, 2007; Wampold, Imel, Bhati, & Johnson Jennings, 2007).

Despite the problems with placebo-type control groups, the evidence produced from designs with such control groups has been used to make claims about how psychotherapy works. In 1994, Lambert and Bergin reviewed 15 meta-analyses to determine the effects of treatment and psychological placebos. Their conclusion was that treatments intended to be therapeutic were superior to psychological placebos (effect size = .48) and that psychological placebos were superior to no treatment (effect size = .42), both medium-sized effects (Cohen, 1988). Advocates of specificity might claim that this is supportive of their position because treatments with specific ingredients outperformed treatments without ingredients. Common factor advocates, however, would say that the controls do not contain all the common factors (e.g., a rationale and therapeutic actions) and that the fact that a condition without a rationale and treatment can produce a sizable effect is evidence for the power of some of the common factors (Wampold, 2001b). Moreover, the difference between treatment with a cogent rationale and therapeutic actions versus one without could be interpreted as the degree to which *any treatment* (i.e., any cogent and convincing treatment delivered by a therapist who intends the treatment to be therapeutic) is important.

Additional meta-analyses of studies using placebo-type controls have attempted to address these issues to establish specificity. Stevens, Hynan, and Allen (2000) included only studies that compared three groups: a specific treatment, a placebo-type control group (which they labeled a *common factor control group*), and a no-treatment control group. They also attempted to control for the credibility of the placebo-type control group. They found larger differences between the specific treatment and the placebo-type control groups and smaller differences between the placebo-type control and no treatment groups than did Lambert and Bergin (1994), results that became more apparent as severity increased. Stevens et al. reached the following conclusions:

> In contrast to Klein's claim that nothing specific is occurring in psychotherapy, we found evidence that the specific components of psychotherapy exceed common factor effects, *as represented by the common factor controls in this meta-analysis* [italics added]. . . . Our meta-analysis clearly indicates that the specific components of psychotherapy exert a beneficial influence over and above the common factors delivered, especially for participants with more severe problems. (pp. 283, 286)

However, as noted, the conclusion about specific effects in psychotherapy made from placebo-type controls is tempered by the fact that, not infrequently, the placebo-type controls contain only some of the common factors thought necessary and that often the common factor controls are not well designed. Baskin et al. (2003) sought to investigate this very issue by classing placebo-type controls into those that were structurally equivalent to the active treatment and those that were not structurally equivalent in terms of therapy duration, format, and therapist training. They found that treatments were superior to structurally inequivalent placebo-type control groups but were not superior to well-designed placebo-type control groups. That is, when placebos approximated in structure the active treatment, their effects were similar to those of the active treatment, providing some evidence that the claims of specificity may be due to aspects of the design of placebo-type control groups.

Establishing the System-Specific Sequence in Psychotherapy

It is has long been recognized that establishing specificity in psychotherapy requires more than a demonstration that active treatments are more effective than placebo-type controls (Rosenthal & Frank, 1956), a point that is made more vital given the ambiguity of placebo-type control studies in psychotherapy. Unfortunately, establishing the system-specific sequence in psychotherapy is tortuously difficult. One of the particular difficulties is that the psychological deficits of mental disorders have not been unambiguously established. The classification systems for mental disorders (e.g., the *Diagnostic and Statistical Manual of Mental Disorders;* American Psychiatric Association, 2000) are objective–descriptive rather than etiological (Widiger & Trull, 2007); that is, mental disorders are determined by patterns of symptoms without establishing particular psychological deficits. The problem this creates for establishing specificity is illustrated by considering panic disorders. The six best explanations for panic have either been falsified or are not falsifiable (Roth, Wilhelm, & Petit, 2005), and therefore attempts to establish that treatments are successful by modifying identified deficits underlying panic are impossible. The lack of established etiological pathways for mental disorders is quite different, say, from that example in which the bacterium *H. pylori* is known to cause peptic ulcers. Despite these problems, there have been many creative efforts to investigate the system-specific sequence in psychotherapy.

A primary way to establish a system-specific sequence is to examine mediating constructs. If Treatment A targets System A to treat a disorder and Treatment B targets System B to treat the same disorder, then both Treatment A and Treatment B may be specific through different systems and both benefit the client. For example, CBT for depression would focus on cognitive distortions and maladaptive attributions, whereas interpersonal therapy (IPT) for depression would focus on relationships and social support. This is an explanation for why there may be generally equivalent outcomes of psychotherapy (i.e., the dodo bird conclusions) and at the same time specificity of the various treatments through different systems (Wampold, 2001b). Investigations could profitably determine the mediating effects of the treatments on their respective systems (i.e., CBT would change cognitions, whereas IPT would change social relationships). Of course, the designs get complex and the results difficult to interpret at times. A few examples are illustrative.

A good example of the examination of mediating systems is the dismantling of CBT for depression by Jacobson et al. (1996). In addition to examining the outcomes of components of CBT (the full package, automatic thoughts, and behavioral activation), they also examined two mediating variables, negative thinking and dysfunctional attributions, which should have been altered as a result of the cognitive components (CBT and to a lesser degree automatic thoughts). Nevertheless, all three treatments, including behavioral activation that contained no cognitive interventions, changed negative thinking and dysfunctional attributions equally. That cognitive variables did not mediate the treatment and depression as expected suggests that CBT is not specific for depression.

In the area of anxiety, Anholt et al. (2008) examined the process of change in CBT and response prevention/exposure for obsessive–compulsive disorder (OCD). Both CBT and response prevention/exposure are effective treatments for OCD. Theoretically, response prevention/exposure is a behavioral treatment focused on the compulsive aspects of OCD, whereas CBT is a cognitive treatment focused on the obsessive aspects. Anholt and colleagues hypothesized that that response prevention/exposure would initially reduce compulsions, which would be followed by a reduction in obsessions, whereas the opposite pattern would be exhibited by CBT. Contrary to predictions, the process of change in both groups was the same, as compulsions changed first in both treatments and change in compulsions was the better predictor of final outcome.

Another salient example of a failure to show mediating effects is found in an analysis of the National Institute of Mental Health (NIMH) Treatment of Depression Collaborative Research Program (TDCRP; Elkin, Parloff, Hadley, & Autry, 1985; Elkin et al., 1989). The two psychotherapy arms, CBT and IPT, were expected to alter dysfunctional attitudes and social adjustment, respectively. However, the expected mediating relationship was not present (Imber et al., 1990):

> Despite different theoretical rationales, distinctive therapeutic proce-
> dures, and presumed differences in treatment processes, none of the
> therapies produced clear and consistent effects at termination of acute
> treatment on measures related to its theoretical origins. This conclu-
> sion applies, somewhat surprisingly, not only to the two psychothera-
> pies but also to pharmacotherapy as practiced in the TDCRP. (p. 357)

It appears that the anticipated mediating effects that are predicted theoretically have not been detected, a conclusion corroborated by a meta-
analysis of studies that included cognitive mediating variables (Oei & Free,
1995). It was found, consistent with the specificity hypothesis, that the cognitive variables did mediate CBT and outcome. However, it was found that
cognitive variables also mediated noncognitive treatments and even phar-
macoptherapies; that is, the cognitive variables mediated the treatment and
outcome in a way that was indistinguishable from CBT.

Other attempts to find specific effects, particularly for CBT, using
mediational-type designs, however, have produced some encouraging evidence for specificity. Research in the area of what has been called *sudden
gains* (Tang & DeRubeis, 1999; Tang, DeRubeis, Beberman, & Pham, 2005;
Tang, DeRubeis, Hollon, Amsterdam, & Shelton, 2007; Tang, Luborsky, &
Andrusyna, 2002) has produced evidence of specificity. A sudden gain is a
large change in symptoms from one session to the next. In the treatment of
depression, clients who showed dramatic change in Beck Depression Inven-
tory scores between sessions were functioning better at the end of treatment
and at various intervals after treatment, and they had fewer relapses as well
(Tang & DeRubeis, 1999; Tang et al., 2002, 2007). Of importance to specificity is that Tang et al. (2005) found that sudden gains in CBT for depression was preceded by substantial cognitive changes in the sessions preceding
the sudden gains. Sudden gains have been found in other treatments (e.g.,
supportive-expressive psychotherapy), but the gains seem to be less stable
and not as related to outcome as they are in CBT (Tang et al., 2002).

It may be that changes in the mediating system are not related to final
outcome, which might be due to the common factors but are related to

longer term outcomes. An argument could be made that fundamental changes in a psychological system provide the client the bases with which to cope with various problems that will occur in his or her life after therapy. The common factors may be sufficient to provide immediate relief, perhaps through a remoralizing process, as suggested by Jerome Frank (Frank & Frank, 1991), but it may be that few lasting changes are made. There is some evidence of this effect. In a study of 35 clients who responded to CBT for depression, it was found that those clients who acquired cognitive coping skills and displayed evidence that they were using CBT principles had lower relapse rates during the year following treatment (Strunk, DeRubeis, Chiu, & Alvarez, 2007). Change in self-esteem, however, was not related to relapse rates.

One of the explanations for the appearance of dodo bird results (i.e., general equivalence of outcomes) is that a given disorder may have multiple etiological pathways. For example, the cause of depression may vary; depression for some clients may be caused by dysfunctional cognitions; for others, by poor social relations; and for still others, by a biological deficit or condition. This is essentially a criticism of diagnostic categories as descriptive rather than etiological (Follette & Houts, 1996). If there are multiple etiological pathways for a given disorder, then a treatment designed for one particular deficit purportedly will be effective only for those clients who have the identified deficit; other treatments, aimed at other deficits, will be effective with other types of clients. This is essentially a matching hypothesis—treatments designed to remediate a particular deficit will be effective when matched with clients who have that deficit.

A number of studies have attempted to test the deficit-matching hypothesis. In the late 1980s, Dance and Neufeld (1988) reviewed matching studies and found little evidence that matching a treatment to clients with a particular deficit produced more benefit. Similarly, B. Smith and Sechrest (1991) claimed that the evidence for this type of matching was "discouraging." Two multisite trials in the area of alcohol use disorders were designed to specifically test matching hypotheses, and neither one corroborated any of the matching hypotheses (Project Match Research Group, 1997; UKATT Research Team, 2007). For example, in the UKATT study, it was hypothesized that clients who were not as ready to change would have better outcomes with motivational enhancement therapy, whereas those with low levels of social support would benefit from social behavior and network therapy, but the outcomes of more than 700 clients provided no support for this hypothesis. Wampold (2001b) reviewed the matching studies and found little evidence to corroborate that psychological treatments matched to deficits are more effective than treatments that are not matched.

Conclusions of Evidence for Specific Effects

Finding evidence for specific effects in psychotherapy is a difficult task, much more difficult than in medicine. For example, designing a placebo that is indistinguishable from the active medication and designing a double-blind placebo trial are feasible in medicine, whereas many issues in comparable design in psychotherapy lead to threats to the validity of the placebo design. Similarly, research in the system-specific sequence in psychotherapy is more complex than it is in medicine because the causes of mental illness are more ambiguous, relatively speaking, as psychological systems are more difficult to observe and study than are biological systems.

Despite the difficulties with research on the issue of specificity, the evidence for specific effects in psychotherapy is relatively sparse. However, because of these difficulties, it is too early to close the door on specific effects. The unambiguous detection of specific effects for a particular disorder would lead to more efficient and effective services.

EVIDENCE FOR COMMON FACTORS

The lack of evidence for specific factors leads to the question of whether the common factors are responsible for the benefits of psychotherapy. The complexity of making inferences from research on the common factors likely is greater than it is for the question of specificity. Most fundamentally, the common factors cannot be experimentally manipulated, so attributions of causation are more contorted than they are in experimental designs. For example, one cannot assign a case to either have a good working alliance or not; the alliance is a variable that is assessed and then correlated with outcome. Thus, does a correlation of alliance and outcome imply that alliance causes outcome, or might outcome cause alliance? Or might a third variable cause both alliance and outcome? And is the alliance–outcome relationship due to the therapist's contribution to the alliance or to the client's contribution to the alliance? That the alliance cannot be manipulated experimentally does not imply that the alliance cannot be causally related to good outcomes; it means only that there are a plethora of threats to the validity of conclusions about causation.

A second difficulty is that the common factors are not discrete ingredients of therapy that can be added to a psychotherapy recipe to create a fine dish. The alliance, which involves agreement about the tasks of therapy, is necessarily tied to the delivery of a treatment. The person of the therapist is a participant in the relationship. The acceptability of the rationale of a treatment (i.e., an explanation of the client's difficulty) both is dependent on the alliance and helps create the alliance. The common factors mutually influence each other over time and thus form a complex system that is difficult to understand, let alone research. Nevertheless, the research evidence for several common factors indicates that they are critically important to the outcome of psychotherapy.

Despite the interconnected nature of the common factors, the research for a select few common factors provides evidence that how a treatment is delivered is more important than which treatment is delivered. It appears that several therapeutic factors are important across the wide variety of existing therapeutic approaches.

The Working Alliance

The concept of the working alliance originated in psychodynamic theory, but in the 1970s the idea became pantheoretical (Horvath & Luborsky, 1993). The modal model of the working alliance (or simply, *the alliance*) consists of three components: the bond between the therapist and the client, agreement about the goals of therapy, and agreement about the tasks of therapy (Hatcher & Barends, 2006; Horvath & Bedi, 2002; Horvath & Luborsky, 1993). The alliance has been characterized as the "the participants' [i.e., therapist's and client's] collaborative, purposeful work"

(Hatcher & Barends, 2006). The interrelatedness of the alliance and other factors is readily apparent in the latter two components, namely agreement about the goals and tasks of therapy (Hatcher & Barends, 2006; Tryon & Winograd, 2002; Wampold, 2007)—there can be no agreement about goals and tasks of therapy without a treatment structure. In the research treatment controls that use minimal responding and no treatment rationale or structure, the alliance is composed entirely of bond, as there are no goals and tasks. Hatcher and Barends succinctly made this point:

> Alliance is a property of all components of therapy, a concept superordinate to these components and not a component itself. Viewing technique and alliance as equivalent components of therapy confuses 2 levels of thinking, as does conflating alliance with the overall therapy relationship. (p. 292)

Despite the theoretical subtleties of the alliance, a predominant question in psychotherapy research has focused on the magnitude of the relationship between the alliance and outcome. The modal design in this area has examined the correlation of the alliance, measured early in psychotherapy (around the third session), and final outcome or change in functioning from pretreatment to termination. Several reviews and meta-analyses have been conducted over the years, and they have found a modest but consistent correlation in the range of .20 (Horvath & Bedi, 2002; Horvath & Symonds, 1991; Martin, Garske, & Davis, 2000). The higher the alliance is at an early session, the better the outcome. Except for initial severity of the client, there is no other variable that has been assessed early in therapy that predicts final outcome better than the alliance.

A number of results accentuate the importance of the alliance. First, the alliance is related to outcome regardless of the type of treatment psychotherapy being offered (Carroll, Nich, & Rounsaville, 1997; Horvath & Bedi, 2002; Krupnick et al., 1994, 1996; Wampold, 2001b), contrary to an expectation that the alliance might be more important in treatments that emphasize the relationship (humanistic or psychodynamic) than in those that are more structured (e.g., CBT). Indeed, there is evidence that the alliance is related to outcome in psychopharmacological treatments (Blatt, Zuroff, Quinlan, & Pilkonis, 1996; Krupnick et al., 1994, 1996). As well, it does not make much difference whether the alliance is rated by therapists, clients, or observers, although slightly higher correlations are found when clients rate the alliance (Martin et al., 2000).

There are some difficulties in interpreting the correlation of alliance and outcome (Crits-Christoph, Gibbons, & Hearon, 2006; DeRubeis, Brotman, & Gibbons, 2005). The central issue is whether it can be concluded that the alliance *caused* the better outcomes. The first problem is that early treatment gains may cause better alliances, and thus it is the early gains in treatment that are creating the correlation between alliance and final outcome. Several attempts have been made to rule out the alliance as a consequence of early gains hypothesis using a variety of complex statistical means. Many studies have found that the early gains are not a confound—that is, the alliance predicts outcome over and above early gains (Baldwin, Wampold, & Imel, 2007; D. N. Klein et al., 2003; Zuroff & Blatt, 2006). However, there is also some evidence that the alliance is a product rather than a cause of outcome.

A second threat to the alliance–outcome connection is that the correlation may be due to the client's contribution to the alliance. Some clients present to therapy with a greater capacity to form interpersonal relationship, perhaps because they have a better attachment history (Mallinckrodt, 1991) and consequently form better alliances with their therapists. And it could be that it is these clients who make better use of therapy and benefit more from it. In this scenario, the client's contribution to the alliance creates better outcomes regardless of the therapist and the therapy. Alternatively, it may well be that it is the therapist's contributions that are important. The therapists who generally form better alliances across a range of clients may well be those who produce better outcomes across a range of clients—that is, effective therapists are effective *because* they are better able to form alliances with their clients. Of course, it might well be an interactive effect as well—some therapists form better alliances with some types of clients, and when there is a good match, better outcomes result.

Baldwin et al. (2007) disentangled the various sources of the alliance (viz., clients, therapists, and interactions) and found that the therapist contributions to the alliance were predictive of outcome whereas client contributions and the interaction of client and therapist were not predictive. That is, the therapists who generally formed better alliances with their clients also had better outcomes. However, for any given therapist, variability in the alliance from one client to another did not predict outcome (see also Trepka, Rees, Shapiro, Hardy, & Barkham, 2004). There is also evidence that training therapists in creating an alliance and working through ruptures in the alliance is effective (Crits-Christoph, Connolly Gibbons, et al., 2006; Hilsenroth, Ackerman, Clemence, Strassle, & Handler, 2002; Safran & Muran, 2000; Safran, Muran, Samstag, & Stevens, 2002). These results are consistent with the discussion in chapter 3—it is critical that therapists elicit collaboration by the client with regard to the explanation provided (i.e., the rationale of therapy) and the tasks of therapy. Thus, the theoretical model, which provides both rationale and tasks, is central to making therapy work.

Although it is difficult to make interpretations about the alliance in therapy for the reasons discussed, there is agreement that it is a critical aspect of all therapy. Even staunch supporters of specificity in psychotherapy would admit that a good alliance is necessary, although not sufficient, for therapeutic change (Barlow, 2004). The evidence seems to indicate that alliance is not attributable to prior change, although there is some disagreement about this. As well, the therapist's contribution to the alliance is what is important with regard to producing better outcomes for that client.

Therapists

One of the tenets of the common factor model of psychotherapy is that the person of the therapist is a critical ingredient (Wampold, 2007). According to this view, some therapists, regardless of the approach undertaken, are more effective than others. The central question is, Do some therapists consistently produce better outcomes than other therapists? If so, what are the characteristics and actions of effective therapists? Historically, the provider of services in many contexts has been ignored as the emphasis has been on the treatment or program (Danziger, 1990; Wampold, 2001a). For example, generally in education, research is aimed at innovations in curriculum or school reform rather than at the teacher who is providing the curriculum (Nye, Konstantopoulos, & Hedges, 2004). In agriculture, the area that spawned many of the statistical methods used in psychology, researchers were interested in farming practices (crop varieties, irrigation, and fertilizers) rather than variations in implementation of these practices by the farmers themselves. In medicine, the drug or procedure has been paramount, and differences in outcomes among physicians were ignored. Psychotherapy similarly has ignored the therapist delivering the approach, particularly in the last few decades (Beutler et al., 2004). Recently, advances in statistical methods (viz., multilevel modeling) have allowed more precise estimates of therapist effects, taking into consideration that clients are nested within therapists (i.e., therapists see many clients using the same treatment, as is the case in clinical trials; see Snijders & Bosker, 1999).

The first source of evidence with regard to therapist effects comes from clinical trials. Because therapists have been ignored, rarely if ever are clinical trials designed to detect therapist effects. Nevertheless, a number of reanalyses have been conducted to estimate how important the thera-pist is. In the early 1990s, Crits-Christoph and colleagues reanalyzed sev-eral clinical trials and found that about 8% of the variance in outcomes *within* treatments was due to the therapists (Crits-Christoph et al., 1991; Crits-Christoph & Mintz, 1991). Again, 8% may seem small but is larger than any other single factor; keeping in mind that psychotherapy vis-à-vis no treatment accounts for 13%, the 8% is apparently quite large.

The NIMH Treatment of Depression Collaborative Research Program (Elkin et al., 1989) was the most extensive clinical trial of psychotherapy ever conducted and provides an example of the importance of therapists. The two psychotherapy arms, CBT and IPT, produced similar outcomes. Indeed, 0% of the variability in outcomes was due to the treatment (CBT vs. IPT). When multilevel models were applied to these data, therapist effects became apparent (Kim, Wampold, & Bolt, 2006)—about 8% of the variability in outcomes *within* each of the psychotherapies was due to the therapist. That is to say, some CBT and some IPT therapists, despite being selected for their expertise, trained to adhere to the respective manuals, and supervised, consistently across their caseloads produced better outcomes than others. The therapist variability in this study was similar in magnitude to the estimates made earlier by Crits-Christoph, although Kim et al.'s result was not without some controversy (Elkin, Falconnier, Martinovich, & Mahoney, 2006; Wampold & Bolt, 2007). Additional analyses of clinical trials also have found sizable therapist effects (e.g., Huppert et al., 2001). Interestingly, in a reanalysis of the TDCRP pharmacoptherapy arm (antidepressants vs. pill placebo), effects attributable to the prescribing psychiatrist became apparent (McKay, Imel, & Wampold, 2006); the psychiatrist met with the client weekly for about 30 minutes. The results indicated that the antidepressant was significantly more effective than the placebo, accounting for about 3% of the variability in outcomes. However, therapist effects were about 9%—and larger than the antidepressant effect. Indeed, the psychiatrists with the highest effects had better outcomes giving the placebo than did the poorer psychiatrists giving the antidepressant! This is all the more surprising because this effect was produced by limited contact between client and psychiatrist.

It might be expected that therapists in practice would be more variable in their outcomes than therapists in clinical trials, where the treatment is manualized, the therapists are selected typically for their skill, and the therapists are trained, monitored, and supervised. Wampold and Brown (2005) estimated therapist effects in a large data set from a managed care context and found that 5% of the variability in outcomes was due to therapist, which is somewhat surprising because this percentage is lower than typically found in clinical trials. However, in naturalistic settings, the heterogeneity of clients makes it more difficult to account for effects. Nevertheless, 5% is clinically important. Wampold and Brown illustrated the therapist effects by ranking therapists in the first time period by the outcomes they produced with their clients and then examining the outcomes in the second time period. The top quartile of therapists in the first time period, identified with as few as three cases, had much better outcomes than the bottom quartile. The pre- to posttreatment effect sizes were twice as large for the top quartile than the bottom quartile—that is, those therapists who attained better outcomes in the first time period had much better outcomes with all types of clients in the second time period. Therapist variability in naturalistic settings has also been found in a number of other studies (Lutz, Leon, Martinovich, Lyons, & Stiles, 2007; Okiishi, Lambert, Nielsen, & Ogles, 2003).

It is clear from the clinical trials and the naturalistic studies that it is how the therapist delivers a particular treatment, rather than the particular treatment, that makes a difference. This raises the inevitable question: What are the characteristics and actions of effective therapists? Depressingly, after decades of research, relatively little is known about the characteristics and actions of effective therapists, a lack that is exacerbated by a decline of research in this area (Beutler et al., 2004). There is little support to suggest that demographics (age, sex, ethnicity), therapy-specific aspects (background, style, choice of interventions), personal characteristics (personality, coping styles, well-being, attitudes, values), or professional training (experience, degree) are related to outcomes.

There is one variable that recently has received some support, and that is the ability to form a therapeutic relationship. Recall that Baldwin et al. (2007) found that more effective therapists are able to form better alliances across a range of clients. Indeed, the differences in average alliances for therapists completely explained the differences in outcomes among the therapists.

There has been additional speculation about therapists who consistently attain good outcomes. It is becoming apparent that social skills are critical—the ability to perceive the emotional state of the client, to express and modulate one's own emotion expression, and to create a collaborative relationship. As well, effective therapists communicate hope that the client will progress, despite any setbacks. These therapists are attuned to client progress—that is, they monitor, either formally through outcome measures or through their interactions with clients, client progress and adjust therapy accordingly (see the following section). Miller, Duncan, and Hubble (2007), relying on the literature on expertise in a variety of cognitive, athletic, and artistic domains, suggested that expert therapists continually use feedback about their performance to improve; deliberate practice in the presence of knowledge about client progress is key.

Customizing Therapy to the Individual Client

One of the common factors discussed earlier is a rationale and treatment that are acceptable to the client. Said another way, the intervention should be compatible with the culture, attitudes, values, and characteristics of the client (Imel & Wampold, 2008; Wampold, 2001b; Wampold, Imel, et al., 2006). There is sufficient evidence from clinical trials that many clients drop out before the end of treatment (Westen & Morrison, 2001), to some extent due to the fact that they did not find the treatment agreeable. Initial engagement in the therapeutic process is critical and has much to do with the client's preference for treatment (Elkin, Yamaguchi, & Arnkoff, 1999; Iacoviello et al., 2007) and expectations about improvement (Connolly Gibbons et al., 2003).

It was noted earlier in this chapter that matching treatment to the particular psychological deficit has not been supported. However, there is some accumulating evidence that matching treatment to personality, coping styles, and motivation do improve completion of therapy and result in better outcomes. Beutler, Moleiro, and Talebi (2002) reviewed literature that suggested that resistant clients fare better with unstructured treatments whereas more compliant clients fare better with relatively more structured treatments. As well, Beutler, Harwood, Alimohamed, and Malik (2002) concluded that clients with externalizing disorders benefit more from treatments that focus on skill building and symptom change, whereas those who are self-critical and avoid emotion benefit relatively more from treatments that focus on interpersonal relations (including with the therapist) and are more insight oriented. Prochaska and Norcross (2002) found that clients who exhibit unreadiness for change benefit from treatments that focus on motivation and do not pressure clients to take immediate action.

Client Factors

One common factor often discussed is the client himself or herself. The notion is a simple one: It is the client who makes therapy work (Bohart & Tallman, 1999; Clarkin & Levy, 2004; Duncan, Miller, & Sparks, 2004; Tallman & Bohart, 1999). A distressed client with sufficient motivation and other requisite resources (e.g., adequate social support, economic resources, and ego strength), it is conjectured, will use therapy with a relatively skilled clinician to make changes in his or her life, regardless of the treatment offered (Tallman & Bohart, 1999). Indeed, many individuals make significant life changes using self-help sources (i.e., without the help of a healer), with nonpsychology persons such as religious figures (ministers, rabbis, mullahs), or with various indigenous or alternative healing practices. According to those who emphasize client factors, the therapist and the treatment provide the necessary conditions for clients, who then use the therapist and the treatment to make desired changes.

From a research perspective, the proportion of variance unaccounted for by various systematic sources, such as treatment or therapist, is by definition client variance. Because much of the variance is unaccounted for, in treatment studies or studies of the common factors, one might be justified in saying that clients are the most important factor in psychotherapy. However, there are several issues when considering client factors in psychotherapy.

Psychotherapy is a transactional endeavor, and it is difficult to parse the various contributions to this process. Common factors, such as the alliance, are created in the interaction, with contributions by both the therapist and the client. Determining whether therapeutic success is due to the therapist's actions or the client's reactions is extremely difficult (see Baldwin et al., 2007, for an attempt to do this in terms of the alliance). In any event, to be useful, knowledge about how clients make use of therapy is necessary. Several characteristics of clients have been shown to be related to better outcomes in psychotherapy, including greater readiness to change, more psychological resources (i.e., greater ego strength), less perfectionism, and higher levels of psychological mindedness (Clarkin & Levy, 2004). As well, clients with greater initial severity are generally more distressed at the end of therapy, although they may have made more progress. However, therapists do not generally select their clients based on the presence of characteristics that predict better outcomes, as therapists want to assist all clients who present, and the absence of characteristics that lead to better prognoses are often the factors that form the basis of the client's problems! Clearly, more research is needed about how clients make use of therapy (Bohart & Tallman, 1999; Clarkin & Levy, 2004; Tallman & Bohart, 1999).

Conclusions About the Common Factors

The review of the literature on common factors was necessarily brief because of the multitude of common factors and the different conceptualizations of the common factors. Research exists on such topics as empathy (Bohart, Elliott, Greenberg, & Watson, 2002), positive regard (Farber & Lane, 2002), expectations (Arnkoff, Glass, & Shapiro, 2002; R. P. Greenberg, Constantino, & Bruce, 2006), and congruence (M. H. Klein, Kolden, Michels, & Chisholm-Stockard, 2002), for example. The research in these and other areas is always complex because of the difficulties inherent in studying a variable that cannot be experimentally manipulated. For example, empathy is associated with better outcomes (Bohart et al., 2002), but without disentangling client and therapist contributions to empathy (i.e., is empathy a therapist-offered condition, or is it elicited from the therapist by the client?), understanding how empathy is involved in the process of psychotherapy is problematic.

Despite the difficulties in researching the common factors, there appears to be relatively strong evidence that common factors are important to the process and outcome of psychotherapy. To believe otherwise might be surprising, as even the most technically minded among us recognize that a client who has a strong bond with his or her therapist and agrees with the goals and tasks of therapy will have a better prognosis than a client who does not. The tension is one of emphasis: Advocates of particular treatments emphasize the effects of specific aspects of the treatment, recognizing that the common factors are necessary, whereas adherents of common factor models emphasize the commonalities, recognizing that a cogent and coherent treatment structure is necessary and that the ingredients are powerful aspects of a treatment.

CONCLUSION

The research evidence has established, without much debate, that psychotherapy is effective. However, with some exceptions, efforts to identify the importance of particular specific ingredients of manualized treatments have not been successful. There is increasing evidence, however, that the alliance and therapists are important factors in psychotherapy. Clearly, additional research is needed to understand how psychotherapy works. A critical issue is determining how psychotherapy delivered in the real world can be improved, both in terms of outcomes of clients in psychotherapy and in terms of delivering psychotherapy to those who are in need of treatment, including culturally diverse groups. It appears that deliberate practice with feedback about performance would be beneficial.

6

Summary

In this book, the role of theory in the process and outcome of psycho-therapy has been discussed. Loosely speaking, psychotherapy is an interpersonal interaction between a therapist and a client aimed at alleviating the client's suffering. But it is not simply a conversation: Therapy has form and substance, created by the therapist's theoretical orientation. A relatively young profession, psychotherapy has been characterized by a rich array of theories. These theories are quite different philosophically, scientifically, and procedurally, as has been discussed in some detail. Psychoanalysis, as developed by Freud, was created in a medical context in Europe and displaced faith-based and spiritual *talk therapies* in the United States. However, the hegemony of psychoanalysis did not last long, as the behaviorists, steeped in learning theory and scientific psychology, sought to lend scientific legitimacy to psychotherapy. Despite a few attempts to integrate behavioral and psychodynamic approaches, much antipathy between the schools existed. After World War II, humanistic approaches, focusing on the meaning of life and phenomenology, became a third force. To add to the array, postmodern approaches have emphasized multicultural counseling, social contexts, and issues of power and oppression. Within each broad category, there are many theories, and more are being developed. To add to this diversity, there are eclectic and integrative approaches. To say the least, the theoretical landscape is vast.

The process of psychotherapy is guided by theory—without theory, there is no psychotherapy. The theory provides the road map for the therapist. An understanding of the client's problems is saturated with theory, and consequently case conceptualizations are theoretically based. Treatment actions similarly are derived from the theory used. In a very profound way, the entire enterprise of psychotherapy, from case conceptualization and treatment planning to each therapist response, emanates from theory.

Given the importance of theory and the multitude of theories, how does one choose a theory to use? There are two perspectives from which to find the answer to this question. First is the therapist perspective. Each therapist needs to select a theory that he or she finds comfortable and appealing. An intellectual appeal flows, most likely, from the philosophy of science that forms the basis of the theory. As well, each theory has a worldview that should be compatible with the attitudes and values of the therapist. Moreover, each theory demands a skill set to deliver—cognitive–behavioral therapy (CBT) involves structure, whereas humanistic theories require a presence in the here and now—and therefore a match between therapist characteristics and theory is needed. Finally, the theory used must be effectively enacted; that is, it is essential that the treatment delivered benefit the client. The therapist perspective can be summarized thusly: The therapist should be passionate about the theory and able to deliver the corresponding treatment effectively.

There are different considerations from the client perspective. Any person presenting to a healer expects an explanation and corresponding actions in the frame of the healing practice. That is to say, psychotherapy clients expect a psychological explanation for their difficulties and some psychological intervention consistent with that explanation. Not all psychological explanations, however, are equally acceptable to a given client—and acceptance by the client is critical. Concordance with the worldview and preferences of the client needs to be considered. For example, some clients respond well to the structure of CBT and prefer the teacher/consultant role of the therapist. Others expect therapy to involve introspection and benefit from the emotional connection to the therapist, and thus they respond better to an experiential/humanistic therapy. In multicultural counseling and psychotherapy, the therapist attempts to understand the client culturally and to provide a culturally relevant or sensitive treatment. The therapist must assess the acceptance of the treatment by the client and be sensitive to client resistance to the treatment; if the client does not respond to a particular theoretical approach, then the therapist must adjust the therapy accordingly. Of course, the skilled therapist presents the rationale and treatment convincingly. Nevertheless, therapists should be competent in providing more than one treatment to accommodate variability in clients' attitudes, values, contexts, and preferences.

There are related issues around the compatibility of the treatment for the therapist and the client. Besides the critical issue of acceptance, the explanation of the client's issues should be adaptive. Often clients present to therapy with explanations for their problems that lead to the conclusion that there is no solution; indeed, clients often present when they feel that their problems cannot be solved and all attempts have failed. For instance, an older engineer who was extremely depressed about his current employment setting returned to school to complete a master's degree. He was doing poorly in classes, and his "imminent" failure would lead to having to remain in his current position, an extremely discouraging outcome in his mind. His explanation for his poor performance involved his age (older than all of the other students by at least a decade) and his lack of intelligence ("These days, students are smarter"). Clearly, the client could not change his age or his intelligence (and neither could the therapist). An alternative, adaptive explanation involved attributing his poor performance to his lack of time to study and disorganized and seemingly uncontrollable personal life. The explanation itself resulted in increased hopefulness— *remoralization* in Jerome Frank's terms or *increased self-efficacy* to complete the necessary tasks in Albert Bandura's terms—because he could take action to address study time and his personal life.

Psychotherapy also involves a treatment that instigates healthy client actions. The treatment, to be successful, must be consistent with the explanation. The particular treatment and client actions differ according to the theory used. For the engineer, CBT was an acceptable treatment, as he was instrumentally oriented, responded to structure, and appreciated the teacher/consultant role; he did not want to be "psychoanalyzed." The therapist was able to use cognitive techniques to change the client's attributions about his poor performance and helped him implement strategies to organize and exert some control over his personal life (assertion skills) to facilitate increased study time and better performance. Of course, the increased control over external events was pleasing to the client regardless of his classroom performance.

What is not important is the truthfulness of the theory. As discussed in this book, *truthiness* is a problematic term because the various psychotherapy theories are derived from incommensurate philosophies of science. What qualifies as truth in the respective theories differs, so there is no resolution possible. The review of the research showed as well that no particular theory or treatment approach appears to be empirically superior to any other, despite concerted attempts to identify particular treatments for particular disorders that consistently produce better outcomes. Despite this evidence, the therapist should believe that the particular theory as he or she is applying it in any particular case is effective, and there is empirical support for this contention.

Decades of clinical trials have shown that psychotherapy is remarkably effective. Generally, it is more effective than many accepted medical practices, is as effective as medication for many mental disorders, is more enduring than medication (i.e., the relapse rates are lower after the treatment is discontinued), and is less resistant to additional courses of treatment than is medication. The average person who receives psychotherapy is better off than about 80% of those who do not. As well, psychotherapy delivered in naturalistic settings seems to produce effects comparable to those achieved in clinical trials. All of this is to reiterate that psychotherapy is remarkably effective.

Again, despite numerous clinical trials comparing psychotherapies intended to be therapeutic (i.e., treatments with legitimate psychological rationales given by trained therapists who have an allegiance to the psychotherapy), it appears that all the approaches are about equally effective. This seems to be true despite the disorder and the nature of the treatment—no one approach is clearly superior to any other. This also seems to true in real-world settings as well as clinical trials. Clearly, treatments that have been tested and found effective in clinical trials have achieved a distinction worth noting, but as discussed in this book, the important question is whether a treatment is effectively delivered by the particular therapist.

Attempts to establish the specificity of particular ingredients of psychotherapy have failed to show that the specific ingredients are necessary to produce the benefits of psychotherapy. When the purported active ingredients are removed from an established treatment, the benefits remain; for example, removing the cognitive components of CBT for depression does not attenuate the benefits. Moreover, it does not appear that particular treatments are mediated by the hypothesized systems; for example, CBT does not seem to be effective because it changes cognitions in ways that other therapies do not. This is not to say that the specific actions in therapy are unneeded; there is research to show that cogent and coherent treatments, consistent with the explanation provided to the client, are absolutely necessary.

If the particular treatment is not critical to outcomes, what makes psychotherapy work? There is evidence that factors common to all therapies are therapeutic, particularly the therapeutic alliance and the therapist. The therapeutic alliance is composed of the bond between therapist and client, agreement about the goals of therapy, and agreement about the tasks of therapy. Essentially, the alliance represents a collaborative relationship between therapist and client resting on the client's acceptance of the explanation provided by the therapist and the concomitant treatment. Research on the alliance has shown that early establishment of the alliance (at about Session 3) is related to the final outcome. Moreover, this relationship is found across therapies, including CBT and behavioral treatments as well as more relational therapies such as humanistic and dynamic therapies; indeed, the alliance is even related to outcomes for psychopharmacological treatments of mental disorders. This research suggests that the particular therapy approach is less important than the collaborative relationship that is built with the client. Keep in mind that the alliance is more than a relationship with an empathic therapist—it is agreement about the goals and tasks of therapy, which depends on acceptance of the explanation and of the treatment.

Throughout this book, the importance of how the therapist delivers a particular treatment has been described as critical. Therapist skill in delivering the treatment is more important that the particular treatment, suggesting that there will be variability in the outcomes produced by therapists. Indeed, it has been found in clinical trials that there is significant variability in the outcomes produced by therapists within treatments—that is to say, some therapists giving the same treatment (say, CBT) consistently produce better outcomes than other therapists. Moreover, variability in outcomes attributable to therapists is much greater than any variability in outcomes attributable to the particular treatment. This is surprising because in clinical trials therapists are typically selected for their skill and are trained, supervised, and monitored to ensure adherence to the treatment protocol. Clinical trials and research in naturalistic settings suggest that therapists are key to creating the benefits of psychotherapy.

The findings of therapist effects raise the question about the characteristics and actions of effective therapists. Interestingly enough, not all that much is known about this critical question. It appears, however, that therapists who achieve better outcomes are better able to form a working alliance across a range of clients. Keeping in mind that alliance formation involves agreement about tasks and goals, facilitating collaboration with the client, regardless of the particular treatment approach, is critical.

Clearly, there are many unresolved issues in the field of psychotherapy, which creates debates among psychotherapy researchers and practitioners. Nevertheless, there is general agreement that improving the quality of mental health services in cost-effective ways is absolutely necessary. Developing new approaches, identifying therapeutic ingredients, and understanding the process of psychotherapy is for naught unless these efforts translate into increased quality of care. Lately, there have been renewed efforts to translate what is known to practice settings. As discussed in chapter 5, an interesting and potentially potent strategy is the provision of feedback to therapists about client progress; regardless of the theoretical approach used, such feedback appears to improve outcomes, particularly for clients at risk for deterioration. Feedback on client progress is also useful to trainees in their development toward being effective therapists.

There is full agreement that therapists need to have a thorough understanding of psychotherapy theory and to be able to use that understanding to benefit their clients. Psychotherapy trainees must appreciate the many issues in the field while focusing on learning various approaches both intellectually and in practice. The process of becoming an effective therapist is a lifelong pursuit involving deliberate practice. The goal is not to select the "right" theory but to learn to use a particular theory—or more likely, theories—effectively. Time is better spent in learning how to be a psychotherapist than in debating the relative merits of the various theories!

The books available in this series present a rich array of theories from which to choose. Readers will resonate with some and find others less appealing. Keep an open mind, and appreciate the diversity of approaches—they all have something important to offer.

References

Acarturk, C., Cuijpers, P., van Straten, A., & de Graaf, R. (2009). Psychological treatment of social anxiety disorder: A meta-analysis. *Psychological Medicine, 39,* 241–254.

Addis, M. E., Hatgis, C., Krasnow, A. D., Jacob, K., Bourne, L., & Mansfield, A. (2004). Effectiveness of cognitive–behavioral treatment for panic disorder versus treatment as usual in a managed care setting. *Journal of Consulting and Clinical Psychology, 72,* 625–635.

Ahn, H., & Wampold, B. E. (2001). A meta-analysis of component studies: Where is the evidence for the specificity of psychotherapy? *Journal of Counseling Psychology, 48,* 251–257.

American Psychiatric Association. (2000). *Diagnostic and statistical manual of mental disorders* (4th ed., text rev.). Washington, DC: Author.

American Psychological Association. (2003). Guidelines on multicultural education, training, research, practice, and organizational change for psychologists. *American Psychologist, 58,* 377–402.

American Psychological Association Presidential Task Force on Evidence-Based Practice. (2006). Evidence-based practice in psychology. *American Psychologist, 61,* 271–285.

Anderson, T., Lunnen, K. M., & Ogles, B. M. (2010). Putting models and techniques in context. In S. D. Miller, B. L. Duncan, M. A. Hubble, & B. E. Wampold (Eds.), *The heart and soul of change: What works in therapy* (2nd ed., pp. 143–167). Washington, DC: American Psychological Association.

Andrews, G., & Harvey, R. (1981). Does psychotherapy benefit neurotic patients? A reanalysis of the Smith, Glass, & Miller data. *Archives of General Psychiatry, 38,* 1203–1208.

Angus, L. E., & McCloud, J. (2007). *Handbook of narrative psychotherapy: Practice, theory, and research.* Thousand Oaks, CA: Sage.

Anholt, G. E., Kempe, P., de Haan, E., van Oppen, P., Cath, D. C., Smit, J. H., et al. (2008). Cognitive versus behavior therapy: Processes of change in the treatment of obsessive-compulsive disorder. *Psychotherapy and Psychosomatics, 77,* 38–42.

Arkowitz, H. (1992). Integrative theories of therapy. In D. K. Freedheim (Ed.), *History of psychotherapy: A century of change* (pp. 261–303). Washington, DC: American Psychological Association.

Arnkoff, D. B., & Glass, C. R. (1992). Cognitive therapy and psychotherapy. In D. K. Freedheim (Ed.), *History of psychotherapy: A century of change* (pp. 657–694). Washington, DC: American Psychological Association.

Arnkoff, D. B., Glass, C. R., & Shapiro, S. J. (2002). Expectations and preferences. In J. C. Norcross (Ed.), *Psychotherapy relationships that work: Therapist contributions and responsiveness to patients* (pp. 335–356). New York: Oxford University Press.

Atkinson, D. R., Bui, U., & Mori, M. (2001). Multiculturally sensitive empirically supported treatments—An oxymoron? In J. G. Ponterotto, J. M. Casas, L. A. Suzuki, & C. M. Alexander (Eds.), *Handbook of multicultural counseling* (2nd ed., pp. 542–574). Thousand Oaks, CA: Sage.

Atkinson, D. R., Worthington, R. L., & Dana, D. M. (1991). Etiology beliefs, preferences for counseling orientations, and counseling effectiveness. *Journal of Counseling Psychology, 38,* 258–264.

Baldwin, S. A., Berkeljon, A., Atkins, D. C., Olsen, J. A., & Nielsen, S. L. (2009). Rates of change in naturalistic psychotherapy: Contrasting dose–effect and good-enough level models of change. *Journal of Consulting and Clinical Psychology, 77,* 203–211.

Baldwin, S. A., Wampold, B. E., & Imel, Z. E. (2007). Untangling the alliance–outcome correlation: Exploring the relative importance of therapist and patient variability in the alliance. *Journal of Consulting and Clinical Psychology, 75,* 842–852.

Barlow, D. H. (2004). Psychological treatments. *American Psychologist, 59,* 869–878.

Barlow, D. H., Craske, M. G., Cerny, J. A., & Klosko, J. S. (1989). Behavioral treatment of panic disorder. *Behavior Therapy, 20,* 261–282.

Barlow, D. H., Gorman, J. M., Shear, M. K., & Woods, S. W. (2000). Cognitive–behavioral therapy, imipramine, or their combination for panic disorder: A randomized controlled trial. *JAMA, 283,* 2529–2536.

Baskin, T. W., Tierney, S. C., Minami, T., & Wampold, B. E. (2003). Establishing specificity in psychotherapy: A meta-analysis of structural equivalence of placebo controls. *Journal of Consulting and Clinical Psychology, 71,* 973–979.

Benish, S., Imel, Z. E., & Wampold, B. E. (2008). The relative efficacy of bona fide psychotherapies of post-traumatic stress disorder: A meta-analysis of direct comparisons. *Clinical Psychology Review, 28,* 746–758.

Bergin, A. E. (1971). The evaluation of therapeutic outcomes. In A. E. Bergin & S. L. Garfield (Eds.), *Handbook of psychotherapy and behavior change* (pp. 217–270). New York: Wiley.

Berman, J. S., Miller, C., & Massman, P. J. (1985). Cognitive therapy versus systematic desensitization: Is one treatment superior? *Psychological Bulletin, 97,* 451–461.

Beutler, L. E., & Clarkin, J. (1990). *Differential treatment selection: Toward targeted therapeutic interventions.* New York: Brunner/Mazel.

Beutler, L. E., Harwood, T. M., Alimohamed, S., & Malik, M. (2002). Functional impairment and coping style. In J. C. Norcross (Ed.), *Psychotherapy relationships that work: Therapist contributions and responsiveness to patients* (pp. 145–170). New York, NY: Oxford University.

Beutler, L. E., Malik, M., Alimohamed, S., Harwood, T. M., Talebi, H., Noble, S., et al. (2004). Therapist variables. In M. J. Lambert (Ed.), *Bergin and Garfield's handbook of psychotherapy and behavior change* (5th ed., pp. 227–306). New York, NY: Wiley.

Beutler, L. E., Moleiro, C. M., & Talebi, H. (2002). Resistance. In J. C. Norcross (Ed.), *Psychotherapy relationships that work: Therapist contributions and responsiveness to patients* (pp. 129–143). New York, NY: Oxford University.

Bike, D. H., Norcross, J. C., & Schatz, D. M. (2009). Processes and outcomes of psychotherapists' personal therapy: Replication and extension 20 years later. *Psychotherapy: Theory, Research, Practice, Training, 46,* 19–31.

Blatt, S. J., Zuroff, D. C., Quinlan, D. M., & Pilkonis, P. A. (1996). Interpersonal factors in brief treatment of depression: Further analysis of the National Institute of Mental Health treatment of depression collaborative research program. *Journal of Consulting and Clinical Psychology, 64,* 162–171.

Bohart, A. C., Elliott, R., Greenberg, L. S., & Watson, J. C. (2002). Empathy. In J. C. Norcross (Ed.), *Psychotherapy relationships that work: Therapist contributions and responsiveness to patients* (pp. 89–87). New York, NY: Oxford University.

Bohart, A. C., & Tallman, K. (1999). *How clients make therapy work: The process of active self-healing.* Washington, DC: American Psychological Association.

Borkovec, T. D. (1990). Control groups and comparison groups in psychotherapy outcome research. *National Institute on Drug Abuse Research Monograph, 104,* 50–65.

Borkovec, T. D., & Costello, E. (1993). Efficacy of applied relaxation and cognitive–behavioral therapy in the treatment of generalized anxiety disorder. *Journal of Consulting and Clinical Psychology, 61,* 611–619.

Boyer, P. (2001). *Religion explained.* New York, NY: Basic Books.

Brom, D., Kleber, R. J., & Defares, P. B. (1989). Brief psychotherapy for post-traumatic stress disorders. *Journal of Consulting and Clinical Psychology, 57,* 607–612.

Brown, L. S. (2006). Still subversive after all these years: The relevance of feminist therapy in the age of evidence-based practice. *Psychology of Women Quarterly, 30,* 15–24.

Caplan, E. (1998). *Mind games: American culture and the birth of psychotherapy.* Berkeley: University of California Press.

Carroll, K. M., Nich, C., & Rounsaville, B. J. (1997). Contribution of the therapeutic alliance to outcome in active versus control psychotherapies. *Journal of Consulting and Clinical Psychology, 65,* 510–514.

Castonguay, L. G. (1993). "Common factors" and "nonspecific variables": Clarification of the two concepts and recommendations for research. *Journal of Psychotherapy Integration, 3,* 267–286.

Chambless, D. L., Baker, M. J., Baucom, D. H., Beutler, L. E., Calhoun, K. S., Daiuto, A., et al. (1998). Update on empirically validated therapies, II. *Clinical Psychologist, 51,* 3–16.

Clarkin, J. F., & Levy, K. N. (2004). The influence of client variables on psychotherapy. In M. J. Lambert (Ed.), *Bergin and Garfield's handbook of psychotherapy and behavior change* (5th ed., pp. 195–226). New York, NY: Wiley.

Clarkin, J. F., Levy, K. N., Lenzenweger, M. F., & Kernberg, O. F. (2007). Evaluating three treatments for borderline personality disorder: A multiwave study. *American Journal of Psychiatry, 164,* 922–928.

Cohen, J. (1988). *Statistical power analysis for the behavioral sciences* (2nd ed.). Hillsdale, NJ: Erlbaum.

Coleman, H. L. K., & Wampold, B. E. (2003). Challenges to the development of culturally relevant empirically supported treatment. In D. B. Pope-Davis, H. L. K. Coleman, W. Liu, & R. Toperek (Eds.), *Handbook of multicultural competencies* (pp. 227–246). Thousand Oaks, CA: Sage.

Comas-Diaz, L. (2000). An ethnopolitical approach to working with people of color. *American Psychologist, 55,* 1319–1325.

Connolly Gibbons, M. B., Crits-Christoph, P., de la Cruz, C., Barber, J. P., Siqueland, L., & Gladis, M. (2003). Pretreatment expectations, interpersonal functioning, and symptoms in the prediction of the therapeutic alliance across supportive-expressive psychotherapy and cognitive therapy. *Psychotherapy Research, 13,* 59–76.

Cottraux, J., Note, I., Yao, S. N., Lafont, S., Note, B., Mollard, E., et al. (2001). A randomized controlled trial of cognitive therapy versus intensive behavior therapy in obsessive compulsive disorder. *Psychotherapy and Psychosomatics, 70,* 288–297.

Critelli, J. W., & Neumann, K. F. (1984). The placebo: Conceptual analysis of a construct in transition. *American Psychologist, 39,* 32–39.

Crits-Christoph, P. (1997). Limitations of the dodo bird verdict and the role of clinical trials in psychotherapy research: Comment on Wampold et al. (1997). *Psychological Bulletin, 122,* 216–220.

Crits-Christoph, P., Baranackie, K., Kurcias, J. S., Carroll, K., Luborsky, L., McLellan, T., et al. (1991). Meta-analysis of therapist effects in psychotherapy outcome studies. *Psychotherapy Research, 1,* 81–91.

Crits-Christoph, P., Connolly Gibbons, M. B., Crits-Christoph, K., Narducci, J., Schamberger, M., & Gallop, R. (2006). Can therapists be trained to improve their alliances? A preliminary study of alliance-fostering psychotherapy. *Psychotherapy Research, 16,* 268–281.

Crits-Christoph, P., Gibbons, M. B., & Hearon, B. (2006). Does the alliance cause good outcome? Recommendations for future research on the alliance. *Psychotherapy: Theory, Research, Practice, Training, 43,* 280–285.

Crits-Christoph, P., & Mintz, J. (1991). Implications of therapist effects for the design and analysis of comparative studies of psychotherapies. *Journal of Consulting and Clinical Psychology, 59,* 20–26.

Cuijpers, P., van Straten, A., Andersson, G., & van Oppen, P. (2008). Psychotherapy for depression in adults: A meta-analysis of comparative outcome studies. *Journal of Consulting and Clinical Psychology, 76,* 909–922.

Cushman, P. (1992). Psychotherapy to 1992: A history situated interpretation. In D. K. Freedheim (Ed.), *History of psychotherapy: A century of change* (pp. 21–64). Washington, DC: American Psychological Association.

Dance, K. A., & Neufeld, R. W. J. (1988). Aptitude–treatment interaction research in the clinic setting: A review of attempts to dispel the "patient uniformity" myth. *Psychological Bulletin, 104,* 192–213.

Danziger, K. (1990). *Constructing the subject: Historical origins of psychological research.* Cambridge, England: Cambridge University Press.

Davidson, P. R., & Parker, K. C. H. (2001). Eye movement desensitization and reprocessing (EMDR): A meta-analysis. *Journal of Consulting and Clinical Psychology, 69,* 305–316.

Dawes, R. M. (1994). *House of cards: Psychology and psychotherapy built on myth.* New York, NY: Free Press.

De Los Reyes, A., & Kazdin, A. E. (2008). When the evidence says, "yes, no, and maybe so": Attending to and interpreting inconsistent findings among evidence-based interventions. *Current Directions in Psychological Science, 17,* 47–51.

DeRubeis, R. J., Brotman, M. A., & Gibbons, C. J. (2005). A conceptual and methodological analysis of the nonspecifics argument. *Clinical Psychology: Science and Practice, 12,* 174–183.

de Waal, F. (2006). *Primates and philosophers: How morality evolved.* Princeton, NJ: Princeton University Press.

Dimidjian, S., Hollon, S. D., Dobson, K. S., Schmaling, K. B., Kohlenberg, R. J., Addis, M. E., et al. (2006). Randomized trial of behavioral activation, cognitive therapy, and antidepressant medication in the acute treatment of adults with major depression. *Journal of Consulting and Clinical Psychology, 74,* 658–670.

Dollard, J., & Miller, N. E. (1950). *Personality and psychotherapy: An analysis in terms of learning, thinking, and culture.* New York, NY: McGraw Hill.

Druss, B. G., Wang, P. S., Sampson, N. A., Olfson, M., Pincus, H. A., Wells, K. B., et al. (2007). Understanding mental health treatment in persons without mental diagnoses: Results from the National Comorbidity Survey Replication. *Archives of General Psychiatry, 64,* 1196–1203.

Duncan, B. L., Miller, S. D., & Sparks, J. A. (2004). *The heroic client: A revolutionary way to improve effectiveness through client-directed, outcome-informed therapy* (rev. ed.). San Francisco, CA: Jossey-Bass.

Eagle, M. N., & Wolitzky, D. L. (1992). Psychoanalytic theories of psychotherapy. In D. K. Freedheim (Ed.), *History of psychotherapy: A century of change* (pp. 109–158). Washington, DC: American Psychological Association.

Elkin, I. (1999). A major dilemma in psychotherapy outcome research: Disentangling therapists from therapies. *Clinical Psychology: Science and Practice, 6,* 10–32.

Elkin, I., Falconnier, L., Martinovich, Z., & Mahoney, C. (2006). Therapist effects in the NIMH Treatment of Depression Collaborative Research Program. *Psychotherapy Research, 16,* 144–160.

Elkin, I., Gibbons, R. D., Shea, M. T., Sotsky, S. M., Watkins, J. T., Pilkonis, P. A., et al. (1995). Initial severity and differential treatment outcome in the National Institute of Mental Health Treatment of Depression Collaborative Research Program. *Journal of Consulting and Clinical Psychology, 63,* 841–847.

Elkin, I., Parloff, M. B., Hadley, S. W., & Autry, J. H. (1985). NIMH Treatment of Depression Collaborative Research Program: Background and research plan. *Archives of General Psychiatry, 42,* 305–316.

Elkin, I., Shea, T., Watkins, J. T., Imber, S. D., Sotsky, S. M., Collins, J. F., et al. (1989). National Institute of Mental Health Treatment of Depression Collaborative Research Program: General effectiveness of treatments. *Archives of General Psychiatry, 46,* 971–982.

Elkin, I., Yamaguchi, J. L., & Arnkoff, D. B. (1999). "Patient–treatment fit" and early engagement in therapy. *Psychotherapy Research, 9,* 437–451.

Elliott, R., & Greenberg, L. S. (2007). The essence of process-experiential/emotion-focused therapy. *American Journal of Psychotherapy, 61*, 241–254.

Elliott, R., Greenberg, L. S., & Lietaer, G. (2004). Research on experiential psychotherapies. In M. J. Lambert (Ed.), *Bergin and Garfield's handbook of psychotherapy and behavior change* (5th ed., pp. 493–539). New York, NY: Wiley.

Emmelkamp, P. M., Visser, S., & Hoekstra, R. J. (1988). Cognitive therapy vs exposure in vivo in the treatment of obsessive-compulsives. *Cognitive Therapy and Research, 12*, 103–114.

Engel, J. (2008). *American therapy: The rise of psychotherapy in the United States.* New York, NY: Gotham Books.

Evans, K. M., Kincade, E. A., Marbley, A. F., & Seem, S. R. (2005). Feminism and feminist therapy: Lessons from the past and hopes for the future. *Journal of Counseling and Development, 83*, 269–277.

Eysenck, H. J. (1952). The effects of psychotherapy: An evaluation. *Journal of Consulting Psychology, 16*, 319–324.

Eysenck, H. J. (1961). The effects of psychotherapy. In H. J. Eysenck (Ed.), *Handbook of abnormal psychology* (pp. 697–725). New York, NY: Basic Books.

Eysenck, H. J. (1966). *The effects of psychotherapy.* New York, NY: International Science Press.

Eysenck, H. J. (1978). An exercise in meta-silliness. *American Psychologist, 33*, 517.

Eysenck, H. J. (1984). Meta-analysis: An abuse of research integration. *Journal of Special Education, 18*, 41–59.

Fancher, R. T. (1995). *Cultures of healing: Correcting the image of American mental health care.* New York, NY: W. H. Freeman.

Farber, B. A., & Lane, J. S. (2002). Positive regard. In J. C. Norcross (Ed.), *Psychotherapy relationships that work: Therapist contributions and responsiveness to patients* (pp. 175–194). New York, NY: Oxford University.

Fishman, D. B., & Franks, C. M. (1992). Evolution and differentiation within behavior therapy: A theoretical and epistemological review. In D. K. Freedheim (Ed.), *History of psychotherapy: A century of change* (pp. 159–196). Washington, DC: American Psychological Association.

Foa, E. B., Hembree, E. A., Cahill, S. P., Rauch, S. A. M., Riggs, D. S., Feeny, N. C., et al. (2005). Randomized trial of prolonged exposure for posttraumatic stress disorder with and without cognitive restructuring: Outcome at academic and community clinics. *Journal of Consulting and Clinical Psychology, 73*, 953–964.

Foa, E. B., Rothbaum, B. O., Riggs, D. S., & Murdock, T. B. (1991). Treatment of post-traumatic stress disorder in rape victims: A comparison between cognitive–behavioral procedures and counseling. *Journal of Consulting and Clinical Psychology, 59*, 715–723.

Follette, W. C., & Houts, A. C. (1996). Models of scientific progress and the role of theory in taxonomy development: A case study of the *DSM*. *Journal of Consulting and Clinical Psychology, 64,* 1120–1132.

Frank, J. D. (1961). *Persuasion and healing: A comparative study of psychotherapy.* Baltimore, MD: Johns Hopkins University Press.

Frank, J. D., & Frank, J. B. (1991). *Persuasion and healing: A comparative study of psychotherapy* (3rd ed.). Baltimore, MD: Johns Hopkins University Press.

Garfield, S. L. (1992). Eclectic pyschotherapy: A common factors approach. In J. C. Norcross & M. R. Goldfried (Eds.), *Handbook of psychotherapy integration* (pp. 169–201). New York, NY: Basic Books.

Garfield, S. L. (1996). Some problems associated with "validated" forms of psychotherapy. *Clinical Psychology: Science and Practice, 3,* 218–229.

Gehan, E., & Lemak, N. A. (1994). *Statistics in medical research: Developments in clinical trials.* New York, NY: Plenum Medical Book.

Gielen, U. P., Draguns, J. G., & Fish, J. M. (Eds.). (2008). *Principles of multicultural counseling and psychotherapy.* New York, NY: Routledge.

Gielen, U. P., Fish, J. M., & Draguns, J. G. (Eds.). (2004). *Handbook of culture, therapy, and healing.* Mahwah, NJ: Erlbaum.

Glass, G. V. (1976). Primary, secondary, and meta-analysis of research. *Educational Researcher, 5,* 3–8.

Gleick, J. (2003). *Isaac Newton.* New York, NY: Pantheon Books.

Gloaguen, V., Cottraux, J., Cucherat, M., & Blackburn, I. (1998). A meta-analysis of the effects of cognitive therapy in depressed patients. *Journal of Affective Disorders, 49,* 59–72.

Goates-Jones, M., & Hill, C. E. (2008). Treatment preference, treatment-preference match, and psychotherapist credibility: Influence on session outcome and preference shift. *Psychotherapy: Theory, Research, Practice, Training, 45,* 61–74.

Goldfried, M. R. (1980). Toward the delineation of therapeutic change principles. *American Psychologist, 35,* 991–999.

Gould, S. J. (1989). The chain of reason vs. the chain of thumbs. *Natural History, 7,* 12–21.

Greenberg, L. S., Elliott, R., & Lietaer, G. (1994). Research on experiential psychotherapies. In A. E. Bergin & S. L. Garfield (Eds.), *Handbook of psychotherapy and behavior change* (4th ed., pp. 509–539). New York, NY: Wiley.

Greenberg, R. P., Constantino, M. J., & Bruce, N. (2006). Are patient expectations still relevant for psychotherapy process and outcome? *Clinical Psychology Review, 26,* 657–678.

Grencavage, L. M., & Norcross, J. C. (1990). Where are the commonalities among the therapeutic common factors? *Professional Psychology: Research and Practice, 21,* 372–378.

Grünbaum, A. (1981). The placebo concept. *Behaviour Research and Therapy, 19,* 157–167.

Hacking, I. (1983). *Representing and interviewing: Introductory topics in the natural philosophy of science.* Cambridge, England: Cambridge University Press.

Hacking, I. (1999). *The social construction of what?* Cambridge, MA: Harvard University Press.

Hall, G. N. (2001). Psychotherapy research with ethnic minorities: Empirical, ethical, and conceptual issues. *Journal of Consulting and Clinical Psychology, 69,* 502–510.

Hansen, N. B., Lambert, M. J., & Forman, E. V. (2002). The psychotherapy dose–response effect and its implications for treatment delivery services. *Clinical Psychology: Science and Practice, 9,* 329–343.

Harmon, C., Lambert, M. J., Smart, D. W., Hawkins, E. J., Nielsen, S. L., Slade, K., et al. (2007). Enhancing outcome for potential treatment failures: Therapist/client feedback and the clinical support tools. *Psychotherapy Research, 17,* 379–392.

Harrington, A. (2008). *The cure within: A history of mind–body medicine.* New York, NY: Norton.

Harris Interactive. (2004). *Therapy in America 2004.* Rochester, NY: Author.

Hatcher, R. L., & Barends, A. W. (2006). How a return to theory could help alliance research. *Psychotherapy: Theory, Research, Practice, Training, 43,* 292–299.

Henry, W. P. (1998). Science, politics, and the politics of science: The use and misuse of empirically validated treatments. *Psychotherapy Research, 8,* 126–140.

Henry, W. P., Schacht, T. E., Strupp, H. H., Butler, S. F., & Binder, J. (1993). Effects of training in time-limited dynamic psychotherapy: Mediators of therapists' responses to training. *Journal of Consulting and Clinical Psychology, 61,* 441–447.

Henry, W. P., Strupp, H. H., Butler, S. F., Schacht, T. E., & Binder, J. (1993). Effects of training in time-limited psychotherapy: Changes in therapist behavior. *Journal of Consulting and Clinical Psychology, 61,* 434–440.

Herbert, J. D., Lilienfeld, S. O., Lohr, J. M., Montgomery, R. W., O'Donohue, W. T., Rosen, G. M., et al. (2000). Science and pseudoscience in the development of eye movement desensitization and reprocessing: Implications for clinical psychology. *Clinical Psychology Review, 20,* 945–971.

Hilsenroth, M. J., Ackerman, S. J., Clemence, A. J., Strassle, C. G., & Handler, L. (2002). Effects of structured clinician training on patient and therapist perspectives of alliance in psychotherapy. *Psychotherapy: Theory, Research, Practice, Training, 39,* 309–323.

Hollon, S. D., Stewart, M. O., & Strunk, D. (2006). Enduring effects for cognitive behavior therapy in the treatment of depression and anxiety. *Annual Review of Psychology, 57,* 285–315.

Horvath, A. O., & Bedi, R. P. (2002). The alliance. In J. C. Norcross (Ed.), *Psychotherapy relationships that work: Therapist contributions and responsiveness to patients* (pp. 37–70). New York, NY: Oxford University.

Horvath, A. O., & Luborsky, L. (1993). The role of the therapeutic alliance in psychotherapy. *Journal of Consulting and Clinical Psychology, 61,* 561–573.

Horvath, A. O., & Symonds, B. D. (1991). Relation between working alliance and outcome in psychotherapy: A meta-analysis. *Journal of Counseling Psychology, 38,* 139–149.

Hubble, M. A., Duncan, B. L., & Miller, S. D. (Eds.). (1999a). *The heart and soul of change: What works in therapy.* Washington, DC: American Psychological Association.

Hubble, M. A., Duncan, B. L., & Miller, S. D. (1999b). Introduction. In M. A. Hubble, B. L. Duncan, & S. D. Miller (Eds.), *The heart and soul of change: What works in therapy* (pp. 1–19). Washington, DC: American Psychological Association.

Huppert, J. D., Bufka, L. F., Barlow, D. H., Gorman, J. M., Shear, M. K., & Woods, S. W. (2001). Therapists, therapist variables, and cognitive behavioral therapy outcomes in a multicenter trial for panic disorder. *Journal of Consulting and Clinical Psychology, 69,* 747–755.

Iacoviello, B. M., McCarthy, K. S., Barrett, M. S., Rynn, M., Gallop, R., & Barber, J. P. (2007). Treatment preferences affect the therapeutic alliance: Implications for randomized controlled trials. *Journal of Consulting and Clinical Psychology, 75,* 194–198.

Imber, S. D., Pilkonis, P. A., Sotsky, S. M., Elkin, I., Watkins, J. T., Collins, J. F., et al. (1990). Mode-specific effects among three treatments for depression. *Journal of Consulting and Clinical Psychology, 58,* 352–359.

Imel, Z. E., Malterer, M. B., McKay, K. M., & Wampold, B. E. (2008). A meta-analysis of psychotherapy and medication in depression and dysthmia. *Journal of Affective Disorders, 110,* 197–206.

Imel, Z. E., & Wampold, B. E. (2008). The common factors of psychotherapy. In S. D. Brown & R. W. Lent (Eds.), *Handbook of counseling psychology* (4th ed., pp. 249–266). New York, NY: Wiley.

Imel, Z. E., Wampold, B. E., Miller, S. D., & Fleming, R. R. (2008). Distinctions without a difference: Direct comparisons of psychotherapies for alcohol use disorders. *Journal of Addictive Behaviors, 22,* 533–543.

Jacobson, N. S., Dobson, K. S., Truax, P. A., Addis, M. E., Koerner, K., Gollan, J. K., et al. (1996). A component analysis of cognitive–behavioral treatment for depression. *Journal of Consulting and Clinical Psychology, 64,* 295–304.

Jones, S. (2008). *The quantum ten: A story of passion, tragedy, ambition, and science.* Oxford, England: Oxford University Press.

Kazdin, A. E. (2000). *Psychotherapy for children and adolescents: Directions for research and practice.* New York, NY: Oxford University Press.

Kernberg, O. F., Yeomans, F. E., Clarkin, J. F., & Levy, K. N. (2008). Transference focused psychotherapy: Overview and update. *International Journal of Psychoanalysis, 89,* 601–620.

Kiesler, D. J. (1994). Standardization of intervention: The tie that binds psychotherapy research and practice. In P. F. Talley, H. H. Strupp & S. F. Butler (Eds.), *Psychotherapy research and practice: Bridging the gap* (pp. 143–153). New York, NY: Basic Books.

Kim, D. M., Wampold, B. E., & Bolt, D. M. (2006). Therapist effects in psychotherapy: A random effects modeling of the NIMH TDCRP data. *Psychotherapy Research, 16,* 161–172.

Klein, D. N., Schwartz, J. E., Santiago, N. J., Vivian, D., Vocisano, C., Castonguay, L. G., et al. (2003). Therapeutic alliance in depression treatment: Controlling for prior change and patient characteristics. *Journal of Consulting and Clinical Psychology, 71,* 997–1006.

Klein, M. H., Kolden, G. G., Michels, J. L., & Chisholm-Stockard, S. (2002). Congruence. In J. C. Norcross (Ed.), *Psychotherapy relationships that work: Therapist contributions and responsiveness to patients* (pp. 195–215). New York, NY: Oxford University.

Klerman, G. L., Weissman, M. M., Rounsaville, B. J., & Chevron, E. S. (1984). *Interpersonal psychotherapy of depression.* New York, NY: Basic Books.

Krupnick, J. L., Elkin, I., Collins, J., Simmens, S., Sotsky, S. M., Pilakonis, P. A., et al. (1994). Therapeutic alliance and clinical outcome in the NIMH Treatment of Depression Collaborative Research Program: Preliminary findings. *Psychotherapy, 3,* 28–35.

Lambert, M. J. (1992). Implications for outcome research for psychotherapy integration. In J. C. Norcross & S. L. Garfield (Eds.), *Handbook of psychotherapy integration* (pp. 94–129). New York, NY: Wiley.

Lambert, M. J., & Bergin, A. E. (1994). The effectiveness of psychotherapy. In A. E. Bergin & S. L. Garfield (Eds.), *Handbook of psychotherapy and behavior change* (4th ed., pp. 143–189). New York, NY: Wiley.

Lambert, M. J., Hansen, N. B., & Finch, A. E. (2001). Patient-focused research: Using patient outcome data to enhance treatment effects. *Journal of Consulting and Clinical Psychology, 69,* 159–172.

Lambert, M. J., Harmon, C., Slade, K., Whipple, J. L., & Hawkins, E. J. (2005). Providing feedback to psychotherapists on their patients' progress: Clinical results and practice suggestions. *Journal of Clinical Psychology, 61,* 165–174.

Lambert, M. J., & Ogles, B. M. (2004). The efficacy and effectiveness of psycho-therapy. In M. J. Lambert (Ed.), *Handbook of psychotherapy and behavior change* (5th ed.). New York, NY: Wiley.

Lambert, M. J., Whipple, J. L., Vermeersch, D. A., Smart, D. W., Hawkins, E. J., Nielsen, S. L., et al. (2002). Enhancing psychotherapy outcomes via providing feedback on client progress: A replication. *Clinical Psychology and Psycho-therapy, 9,* 91–103.

Landman, J. T., & Dawes, R. M. (1982). Psychotherapy outcome: Smith and Glass' conclusions stand up under scrutiny. *American Psychologist, 37,* 504–516.

Langman, P. F. (1997). White culture, Jewish culture, and the origins of psycho-therapy. *Psychotherapy, 34,* 207–218.

Langreth, R. (2007, April 9). Patient, fix thyself. *Forbes,* pp. 80–86.

Latour, B. (1999). *Pandora's hope: Essays on the reality of science studies.* Cambridge, MA: Harvard University Press.

Lazarus, A. A. (1981). *The practice of multimodal therapy.* New York, NY: McGraw-Hill.

Leichsenring, F., & Leibing, E. (2003). The effectiveness of psychodynamic ther-apy and cognitive behavior therapy in the treatment of personality disorders: A meta-analysis. *American Journal of Psychiatry, 160,* 1223–1231.

Leykin, Y., Amsterdam, J. D., DeRubeis, R. J., Gallop, R., Shelton, R. C., & Hol-lon, S. D. (2007). Progressive resistance to a selective serotonin reuptake inhibitor but not to cognitive therapy in the treatment of major depression. *Journal of Consulting and Clinical Psychology, 75,* 267–276.

Linehan, M. M. (1993). *Cognitive–behavioral treatment of borderline personality disorder.* New York, NY: Guilford Press.

Linehan, M. M., Comtois, K. A., Murray, A., Brown, M., Gallop, R. J., Heard, H. L., et al. (2006). Two-year randomized controlled trial and follow-up of dialectical behavior therapy vs therapy by experts for suicidal behaviors and borderline personality disorder. *Archives of General Psychiatry, 63,* 757–766.

Luborsky, L., Diguer, L., Seligman, D. A., Rosenthal, R., Krause, E. D., Johnson, S., et al. (1999). The researcher's own therapy allegiances: A "wild card" in comparisons of treatment efficacy. *Clinical Psychology: Science and Practice, 6,* 95–106.

Luborsky, L., McLellan, A. T., Diguer, L., Woody, G., & Seligman, D. A. (1997). The psychotherapist matters: Comparison of outcomes across twenty-two therapists and seven patient samples. *Clinical Psychology: Science and Practice, 4,* 53–65.

Luborsky, L., McLellan, A. T., Woody, G., O'Brien, C. P., & Auerbach, A. (1985). Therapist success and its determinants. *Archives of General Psychiatry, 42,* 602–611.

Luborsky, L., Singer, B., & Luborsky, L. (1975). Comparative studies of psycho-therapies: Is it true that "Everyone has won and all must have prizes"? *Archives of General Psychiatry, 32,* 995–1008.

Lutz, W., Leon, S. C., Martinovich, Z., Lyons, J. S., & Stiles, W. B. (2007). Thera-pist effects in outpatient psychotherapy: A three-level growth curve approach. *Journal of Counseling Psychology, 54,* 32–39.

Makari, G. (2008). *Revolution in mind: The creation of psychoanalysis.* New York, NY: HarperCollins.

Mallinckrodt, B. (1991). Clients' representations of childhood emotional bonds with parents, social support, and formation of the working alliance. *Journal of Counseling Psychology, 38,* 401–409.

Martin, D. J., Garske, J. P., & Davis, M. K. (2000). Relation of the therapeutic alliance with outcome and other variables: A meta-analytic review. *Journal of Consulting and Clinical Psychology, 68,* 438–450.

McDonagh, A., Friedman, M., McHugo, G., Ford, J., Sengupta, A., Mueser, K., et al. (2005). Randomized trial of cognitive–behavioral therapy for chronic posttraumatic stress disorder in adult female survivors of childhood sexual abuse. *Journal of Consulting and Clinical Psychology, 73,* 515–524.

McKay, K. M., Imel, Z. E., & Wampold, B. E. (2006). Psychiatrist effects in the psychopharmacological treatment of depression. *Journal of Affective Disorders, 16,* 236–242.

Meichenbaum, D. (1986). Cognitive–behavior modification. In F. H. Kanfer & A. P. Goldstein (Eds.), *Helping people change: A textbook of methods* (3rd ed., pp. 346–380). New York, NY: Pergamon Press.

Meltzoff, J., & Kornreich, M. (1970). *Research in psychotherapy.* Chicago, IL: Aldine.

Messer, S. B. (2004). Evidence-based practice: Beyond empirically supported treatments. *Professional Psychology: Research and Practice, 35,* 580–588.

Miller, S. D., Duncan, B. L., & Hubble, M. A. (2005). Outcome-informed clinical work. In J. C. Norcross & M. R. Goldfried (Eds.), *Handbook of psychotherapy integration* (2nd ed., pp. 84–102). New York, NY: Oxford University Press.

Miller, S. D., Duncan, B., & Hubble, M. (2007, November/December). Super shrinks: Who are they? What can we learn from them? *Psychotherapy Networker,* pp. 27–56.

Miller, S. D., Wampold, B. E., & Varhely, K. (2008). Direct comparisons of treat-ment modalities for youth disorders: A meta-analysis. *Psychotherapy Research, 18,* 5–14.

Milrod, B., Leon, A. C., Busch, F., Rudden, M., Schwalberg, M., Clarkin, J., et al. (2007). A randomized controlled clinical trial of psychoanalytic psychotherapy for panic disorder. *American Journal of Psychiatry, 164,* 265–272.

Minami, T., Serlin, R. C., Wampold, B. E., Kircher, J., & Brown, G. S. (2008). Using clinical trials to benchmark effects produced in clinical practice. *Quality and Quantity, 42*, 513–525.

Minami, T., & Wampold, B. E. (2008). Adult psychotherapy in the real world. In W. B. Walsh (Ed.), *Biennial review of counseling psychology* (Vol. 1, pp. 27–45). New York, NY: Taylor and Francis.

Minami, T., Wampold, B. E., Serlin, R. C., Hamilton, E., Brown, G. S., & Kircher, J. (2008). Benchmarking the effectiveness of psychotherapy treatment for adult depression in a managed care environment: A preliminary study. *Journal of Consulting and Clinical Psychology, 76*, 116–124.

Minami, T., Wampold, B. E., Serlin, R. C., Kircher, J. C., & Brown, G. S. J. (2007). Benchmarks for psychotherapy efficacy in adult major depression. *Journal of Consulting and Clinical Psychology, 75*, 232–243.

Mitte, K. (2005). Meta-analysis of cognitive–behavioral treatments for generalized anxiety disorder: A comparison with pharmacotherapy. *Psychological Bulletin, 131*, 785–795.

Mitte, K., Noack, P., Steil, R., & Hautzinger, M. (2005). A meta-analytic review of the efficacy of drug treatment in generalized anxiety disorder. *Journal of Clinical Psychopharmacology, 25*, 141–150.

Mosher, P. W., & Richards, A. (2005). The history of membership and certification in the APsaA: Old demons, new debates. *Psychoanalytic Review, 92*, 865–894.

Moyers, T. B., Miller, W. R., & Hendrickson, S. M. L. (2005). How does motivational interviewing work? Therapist interpersonal skill predicts client involvement within motivational interviewing sessions. *Journal of Consulting and Clinical Psychology, 73*, 590–598.

Murdock, N. L. (2008). *Theories of counseling and psychotherapy: A case approach* (2nd ed.). Upper Saddle River, NJ: Merrill.

Norcross, J. C., Bike, D. H., & Evans, K. L. (2009). The therapist's therapist: A replication and extension 20 years later. *Psychotherapy: Theory, Research, Practice, Training, 46*, 32–41.

Norcross, J. C., & Goldfried, M. R. (1992). *Handbook of psychotherapy integration.* New York, NY: Basic Books.

Norcross, J. C., & Goldfried, M. R. (2005). *Handbook of psychotherapy integration* (2nd ed.). New York, NY: Oxford University Press.

Norcross, J. C., Hedges, M., & Castle, P. H. (2002). Psychologists conducting psychotherapy in 2001: A study of the Division 29 membership. *Psychotherapy: Theory, Research, Practice, Training, 39*, 97–102.

Norcross, J. C., & Newman, C. F. (1992). Psychotherapy integration: Setting the context. In J. C. Norcross & M. R. Goldfried (Eds.), *Handbook of psychotherapy integration* (pp. 3–45). New York, NY: Basic Books.

Norcross, J. C., & Tomcho, T. J. (1994). Great books in psychology: Three studies in search of a consensus. *Teaching of Psychology, 21,* 86–90.

Nye, B., Konstantopoulos, S., & Hedges, L. V. (2004). How large are teacher effects? *Educational Evaluation and Policy Analysis, 26,* 237–257.

Oei, T. P. S., & Free, M. L. (1995). Do cognitive behaviour therapies validate cognitive models of mood disorders? A review of the empirical evidence. *International Journal of Psychology, 30,* 145–179.

Okiishi, J., Lambert, M. J., Nielsen, S. L., & Ogles, B. M. (2003). Waiting for supershrink: An empirical analysis of therapist effects. *Clinical Psychology & Psychotherapy, 10,* 361–373.

Olfson, M., Marcus, S. C., Druss, B., Elinson, L., Tanielian, T., & Rincus, H. A. (2002). National trends in the outpatient treatment of depression. *JAMA, 287,* 203–209.

Ollendick, T. H., & King, N. J. (2006). Empirically supported treatments typically produce outcomes superior to non-empirically supported treatment therapies. In J. C. Norcross, L. E. Beutler, & R. F. Levant (Eds.), *Evidence-based practices in mental health: Debate and dialogue on the fundamental questions* (pp. 308–317). Washington, DC: American Psychological Association.

Orlinsky, D. E., & Howard, K. I. (1986). Process and outcome in psychotherapy. In S. L. Garfield & A. E. Bergin (Eds.), *Handbook of psychotherapy and behavior change* (3rd ed., pp. 311–381). New York, NY: Wiley.

Orlinsky, D. E., & Ronnestad, M. H. (2005). *How psychotherapists develop: A study of therapeutic work and professional growth.* Washington, DC: American Psychological Association.

Paul, G. L. (1969). Behavior modification research: Design and tactics. In C. M. Franks (Ed.), *Behavior therapy: Appraisal and status* (pp. 29–62). New York, NY: McGraw-Hill.

Pedersen, P. (1990). The multicultural perspective as a fourth force in counseling. *Journal of Mental Health Counseling, 12,* 93–95.

Pedersen, P. (2001). Multiculturalism and the paradigm shift in counseling: Controversies and alternative futures. *Canadian Journal of Counselling, 35,* 15–25.

Pilgram, D. (1997). *Psychotherapy and society.* Thousand Oaks, CA: Sage.

Ponterotto, J. G., Casas, J. M., Suzuki, L. A., & Alexander, C. M. (Eds.). (1995). *Handbook of multicultural counseling.* Thousand Oaks, CA: Sage.

Pritz, A. (2002). *Globalized psychotherapy.* Vienna, Austria: Facultas Verlags.

Prochaska, J. O., & Norcross, J. C. (2002). Stages of change. In J. C. Norcross (Ed.), *Psychotherapy relationships that work: Therapist contributions and responsiveness to patients* (pp. 303–313). New York, NY: Oxford University.

Project Match Research Group. (1997). Matching alcoholism treatments to client heterogeneity: Project Match posttreatment drinking outcomes. *Journal of Studies on Alcohol, 58,* 7–29.

Rachman, S. (1971). *The effects of psychotherapy.* Oxford, England: Pergamon Press.

Rachman, S., & Wilson, G. T. (1980). *The effects of psychological therapy* (2nd ed.). New York, NY: Pergamon Press.

Resick, P. A., Galovski, T. E., Uhlmansiek, M. O., Scher, C. D., Clum, G. A., & Young-Xu, Y. (2008). A randomized clinical trial to dismantle components of cognitive processing therapy for posttraumatic stress disorder in female victims of interpersonal violence. *Journal of Consulting and Clinical Psychology, 76,* 243–258.

Rice, L. N., & Greenberg, L. S. (1992). Humanistic approaches to psychotherapy. In D. K. Freedheim (Ed.), *History of psychotherapy: A century of change* (pp. 197–224). Washington, DC: American Psychological Association.

Robinson, L. A., Berman, J. S., & Neimeyer, R. A. (1990). Psychotherapy for the treatment of depression: A comprehensive review of controlled outcome research. *Psychological Bulletin, 108,* 30–49.

Rosa-Alcázar, A. I., Sánchez-Meca, J., Gómez-Conesa, A., & Marín-Martínez, F. (2008). Psychological treatments of obsessive–compulsive disorders: A meta-analysis. *Clinical Psychology Review, 28,* 1310–1325.

Rosenthal, D., & Frank, J. D. (1956). Psychotherapy and the placebo effect. *Psychological Bulletin, 53,* 294–302.

Rosenzweig, S. (1936). Some implicit common factors in diverse methods of psychotherapy: "At last the Dodo said, 'Everybody has won and all must have prizes.'" *American Journal of Orthopsychiatry, 6,* 412–415.

Roth, W. T., Wilhelm, F. H., & Petit, D. (2005). Are current theories of panic falsifiable? *Psychological Bulletin, 131,* 171–192.

Rothbaum, B. O., Astin, M. C., & Marsteller, F. (2005). Prolonged exposure versus eye movement desensitization and reprocessing (EMDR) for PTSD rape victims. *Journal of Traumatic Stress, 18,* 607–616.

Sackett, D. L., Straus, S. E., Richardson, W. S., Rosenberg, W., & Haynes, R. B. (2000). *Evidence based medicine: How to practice and teach EBM* (2nd ed.). London, England: Churchill Livingstone.

Safran, J. D., & Muran, J. C. (2000). *Negotiating the therapeutic alliance.* New York, NY: Guilford Press.

Safran, J. D., Muran, J. C., Samstag, L. W., & Stevens, C. (2002). Repairing alliance ruptures. In J. C. Norcross (Ed.), *Psychotherapy relationships that work: Therapist contributions and responsiveness to patients* (pp. 235–254). New York, NY: Oxford University.

Santayana, G. (1905). The life of reason (Vol. 1). New York, NY: Scribner's.

Schneider, K. (2008). *Existential-integrative psychotherapy: Guideposts to the core of practice.* New York, NY: Routledge.

Schulte, D. (2007). New law for psychological psychotherapies in Germany—Its rules and consequences. *Mental Health and Learning Disabilities Research and Practice, 4,* 219 230.

Shadish, W. R., Matt, G. E., Navarro, A. M., Siegle, G., Crits-Christoph, P., Hazelrigg, M. D., et al. (1997). Evidence that therapy works in clinically representative conditions. *Journal of Consulting and Clinical Psychology, 65,* 355–365.

Shadish, W. R., Navarro, A. M., & Matt, G. E. (2000). The effects of psychological therapies in clinically representative conditions: A meta-analysis. *Psychological Bulletin, 126,* 512–529.

Shadish, W. R., & Sweeney, R. B. (1991). Mediators and moderators in meta-analysis: There's a reason we don't let dodo birds tell us which psychotherapies should have prizes. *Journal of Consulting and Clinical Psychology, 59,* 883–893.

Shapiro, A. K., & Morris, L. A. (1978). The placebo effect in medical and psychological therapies. In S. L. Garfield & A. E. Bergin (Eds.), *Handbook of psychotherapy and behavior change* (2nd ed., pp. 369–410). New York, NY: Wiley.

Shapiro, A. K., & Shapiro, E. S. (1997). *The powerful placebo: From ancient priest to modern medicine.* Baltimore, MD: Johns Hopkins University Press.

Shapiro, D. A., & Shapiro, D. (1982a). Meta-analysis of comparative therapy outcome research: A critical appraisal. *Behavioural Psychotherapy, 10,* 4–25.

Shapiro, D. A., & Shapiro, D. (1982b). Meta-analysis of comparative therapy outcome studies: A replication and refinement. *Psychological Bulletin, 92,* 581–604.

Shapiro, F. (1989). Efficacy of eye movement desensitization procedure in the treatment of traumatic memories. *Journal of Traumatic Stress, 2,* 199–203.

Shepherd, M. (1993). The placebo: From specificity to the non-specific and back. *Psychological Medicine, 23,* 569–578.

Siev, J., & Chambless, D. L. (2007). Specificity of treatment effects: Cognitive therapy and relaxation for generalized anxiety and panic disorders. *Journal of Consulting and Clinical Psychology, 75,* 513–522.

Simons, M., Schneider, S., & Herpertz-Dahlmann, B. (2006). Metacognitive therapy versus exposure and response prevention for pediatric obsessive–compulsive disorder. *Psychotherapy and Psychosomatics, 75,* 257–264.

Singer, M. T., & Lalich, J. (1996). *"Crazy" therapies: What are they? Do they work?* New York, NY: Jossey-Bass.

Smith, B., & Sechrest, L. (1991). Treatment of aptitude × treatment interactions. *Journal of Consulting and Clinical Psychology, 59,* 233–244.

Smith, M. L., & Glass, G. V. (1977). Meta-analysis of psychotherapy outcome studies. *American Psychologist, 32,* 752–760.

Smith, M. L., Glass, G. V., & Miller, T. I. (1980). *The benefits of psychotherapy.* Baltimore, MD: Johns Hopkins University Press.

Snijders, T., & Bosker, R. (1999). *Multilevel analysis: An introduction to basic and advanced multilevel modeling.* London, England: Sage.

Spiegel, A. (2004, June 2). *Cognitive behavior therapy: Thinking positive* [Radio broadcast]. Washington, DC: National Public Radio. Retrieved September 9, 2009, from http://www.npr.org/templates/story/story.php?storyId=1920052

Spielmans, G. I., Pasek, L. F., & McFall, J. P. (2007). What are the active ingredients in cognitive and behavioral psychotherapy for anxious and depressed children? A meta-analytic review. *Clinical Psychology Review, 27,* 642–654.

Stevens, S. E., Hynan, M. T., & Allen, M. (2000). A meta-analysis of common factor and specific treatment effects across domains of the phase model of psychotherapy. *Clinical Psychology: Science and Practice, 7,* 273–290.

Stiles, W. B., Barkham, M., Connell, J., & Mellor-Clark, J. (2008). Responsive regulation of treatment duration in routine practice in United Kingdom primary care settings: Replication in a larger sample. *Journal of Consulting and Clinical Psychology, 76,* 298–305.

Stiles, W. B., Barkham, M., Mellor-Clark, J., & Connell, J. (2008). Effectiveness of cognitive–behavioural, person-centred, and psychodynamic therapies in UK primary-care routine practice: Replication in a larger sample. *Psychological Medicine, 38,* 677–688.

Stiles, W. B., Barkham, M., Twigg, E., Mellor-Clark, J., & Cooper, M. (2006). Effectiveness of cognitive–behavioural, person-centred and psychodynamic therapies as practised in UK National Health Service settings. *Psychological Medicine, 36,* 555–566.

Strauss, A., & Corbin, J. (1998). *Basics of qualitative research: Techniques and procedures for developing grounded theory* (2nd ed.). Thousand Oaks, CA: Sage.

Stricker, G., & Gold, J. R. (1996). Psychotherapy integration: An assimilative, psychodynamic approach. *Clinical Psychology: Science and Practice, 3,* 47–58.

Strunk, D. R., DeRubeis, R. J., Chiu, A. W., & Alvarez, J. (2007). Patients' competence in and performance of cognitive therapy skills: Relation to the reduction of relapse risk following treatment for depression. *Journal of Consulting and Clinical Psychology, 75,* 523–530.

Sue, S. (1998). In search of cultural competence in psychotherapy and counseling. *American Psychologist, 53,* 440–448.

Sue, S., & Lam, A. G. (2002). Cultural and demographic diversity. In J. C. Norcross (Ed.), *Psychotherapy relationships that work: Therapist contributions and responsiveness of patients* (pp. 401–421). New York, NY: Oxford University Press.

Sue, S., Zane, N., & Young, K. (1994). Research on psychotherapy with cultur-ally diverse populations. In A. E. Bergin & S. L. Garfield (Eds.), *Handbook of psychotherapy and behavior change* (4th ed., pp. 783–817). New York, NY: Wiley.

Tallman, K., & Bohart, A. C. (1999). The client as a common factor: Clients as self-healers. In M. Hubble, B. Duncan, & S. D. Miller (Eds.), *The heart and soul of therapy: What works in therapy* (pp. 91–131). Washington, DC: American Psychological Association.

Tang, T. Z., & DeRubeis, R. J. (1999). Sudden gains and critical sessions in cognitive–behavioral therapy for depression. *Journal of Consulting and Clinical Psychology, 67,* 894–904.

Tang, T. Z., DeRubeis, R. J., Beberman, R., & Pham, T. (2005). Cognitive changes, critical sessions, and sudden gains in cognitive–behavioral therapy for depres-sion. *Journal of Consulting and Clinical Psychology, 73,* 168–172.

Tang, T. Z., DeRubeis, R. J., Hollon, S. D., Amsterdam, J. D., & Shelton, R. C. (2007). Sudden gains in cognitive therapy of depression and depression relapse/recurrence. *Journal of Consulting and Clinical Psychology, 75,* 404–408.

Tang, T. Z., Luborsky, L., & Andrusyna, T. (2002). Sudden gains in recovering from depression: Are they also found in psychotherapies other than cognitive–behavioral therapy? *Journal of Consulting and Clinical Psychology, 70,* 444–447.

Tarrier, N., Pilgrim, H., Sommerfield, C., Faragher, B., Reynolds, M., Graham, E., et al. (1999). A randomized trial of cognitive therapy and imaginal exposure in the treatment of chronic posttraumatic stress disorder. *Journal of Consulting and Clinical Psychology, 67,* 13–18.

Task Force on Promotion and Dissemination of Psychological Procedures. (1995). Training in and dissemination of empirically-validated psychological treatment: Report and recommendations. *Clinical Psychologist, 48,* 2–23.

Taylor, E. (1999). *Shadow culture: Psychology and spirituality in America.* Wash-ington, DC: Counterpoint.

Torrey, E. F. (1972). What Western psychotherapists can learn from witchdoctors. *American Journal of Orthopsychiatry, 42.*

Trepka, C., Rees, A., Shapiro, D. A., Hardy, G. E., & Barkham, M. (2004). Ther-apist competence and outcome in cognitive therapy for depression. *Cognitive Therapy and Research, 28,* 143–157.

Tryon, G. S., & Winograd, G. (2002). Goal consensus and collaboration. In J. C. Norcross (Ed.), *Psychotherapy relationships that work: Therapist contributions and responsiveness to patients* (pp. 109–125). New York, NY: Oxford University.

UKATT Research Team. (2007). UK alcohol treatment trial: Client–treatment matching effects. *Addiction, 103,* 228–238.

VandenBos, G. R., Cummings, N. A., & DeLeon, P. H. (1992). A century of psychotherapy: Economic and environmental influences. In D. K. Freedheim (Ed.), *A history of psychotherapy: A century of change* (pp. 65–102). Washington, DC: American Psychological Association.

Van Oppen, P., de Haan, E., Van Balkom, A. J. L. M., & Spinhoven, P. (1995). Cognitive therapy and exposure in vivo in the treatment of obsessive compulsive disorder. *Behaviour Research and Therapy, 33,* 379–390.

Wachtel, P. L. (1977). *Psychoanalysis and behavior therapy: Toward an integration.* New York, NY: Basic Books.

Wampold, B. E. (1997). Methodological problems in identifying efficacious psychotherapies. *Psychotherapy Research, 7,* 21–43.

Wampold, B. E. (2001a). Contextualizing psychotherapy as a healing practice: Culture, history, and methods. *Applied and Preventive Psychology, 10,* 69–86.

Wampold, B. E. (2001b). *The great psychotherapy debate: Model, methods, and findings.* Mahwah, NJ: Erlbaum.

Wampold, B. E. (2005). Locating and describing psychotherapy integration: How much longer until we are there? *PsycCRITIQUES, 50.*

Wampold, B. E. (2006). The psychotherapist. In J. C. Norcross, L. E. Beutler, & R. F. Levant (Eds.), *Evidence-based pratices in mental health: Debate and dialogues on the fundamental questions* (pp. 200–208). Washington, DC: American Psychological Association.

Wampold, B. E. (2007). Psychotherapy: *The* humanistic (and effective) treatment. *American Psychologist, 62,* 857–873.

Wampold, B. E., & Bhati, K. S. (2004). Attending to the omissions: A historical examination of the evidenced-based practice movement. *Professional Psychology: Research and Practice, 35,* 563–570.

Wampold, B. E., & Bolt, D. M. (2007). The consequences of "anchoring" in longitudinal multilevel models: Bias in the estimation of patient variability and therapist effects. *Psychotherapy Research, 17,* 509–514.

Wampold, B. E., & Brown, G. S. (2005). Estimating therapist variability: A naturalistic study of outcomes in managed care. *Journal of Consulting and Clinical Psychology, 73,* 914–923.

Wampold, B. E., Goodheart, C. D., & Levant, R. F. (2007). Evidence-based practice in psychology: Clarification and elaboration. *American Psychologist, 62,* 616–618.

Wampold, B. E., Imel, Z. E., Bhati, K. S., & Johnson Jennings, M. D. (2007). Insight as a common factor. In L. G. Castonguay & C. E. Hill (Eds.), *Insight in psychotherapy* (pp. 119–135). Washington, DC: American Psychological Association.

Wampold, B. E., Lichtenberg, J. W., & Waehler, C. A. (2002). Principles of empirically supported interventions in counseling psychology. *Counseling Psychologist,
30,* 197–207.

Wampold, B. E., Minami, T., Baskin, T. W., & Tierney, S. C. (2002). A meta-
(re)analysis of the effects of cognitive therapy versus "other therapies" for depression. *Journal of Affective Disorders, 68,* 159–165.

Wampold, B. E., Mondin, G. W., Moody, M., Stich, F., Benson, K., & Ahn, H.
(1997). A meta-analysis of outcome studies comparing bona fide psychotherapies: Empirically, "All must have prizes." *Psychological Bulletin, 122,* 203–215.

Wampold, B. E., Ollendick, T. H., & King, N. J. (2006). Do therapies designated
as empirically supported treatments for specific disorders produce outcomes
superior to non-empirically supported treatment therapies? In J. C. Norcross,
L. E. Beutler, & R. F. Levant (Eds.), *Evidence-based practices in mental health:
Debate and dialogue on fundamental questions* (pp. 299–328). Washington,
DC: American Psychological Association.

Wang, P. S., Demler, O., Olfson, M., Pincus, H. A., Wells, K. B., & Kessler, R. C.
(2006). Changing profiles of service sectors used for mental health care in the
United States. *American Journal of Psychiatry, 163,* 1187–1198.

Wang, P. S., Lane, M., Olfson, M., Pincus, H. A., Wells, K. B., & Kessler, R. C.
(2005). Twelve-month use of mental health services in the United States:
Results from the National Comorbidity Survey Replication. *Archives of General
Psychiatry, 62,* 629–640.

Watson, J. B., & Rayner, R. (1920). Conditioned emotional reactions. *Experimental Psychology, 3,* 1–14.

Watson, J. C., Gordon, L. B., Stermac, L., Kalogerakos, F., & Steckley, P. (2003).
Comparing the effectiveness of process-experiential with cognitive–behavioral
psychotherapy in the treatment of depression. *Journal of Consulting and Clinical Psychology, 71,* 773–781.

Weersing, V. R., & Weisz, J. R. (2002). Community clinic treatment of depressed
youth: Benchmarking usual care against CBT clinical trials. *Journal of Consulting and Clinical Psychology, 70,* 299–310.

Weinberger, J., & Rasco, C. (2007). Empirically supported common factors. In
S. G. Hofmann & J. Weinberger (Eds.), *The art and science of psychotherapy*
(pp. 103–129). New York, NY: Routledge/Taylor & Francis Group.

Weinberger, J., & Westen, D. (2001). Science and psychodynamics: From arguments about Freud to data. *Psychological Inquiry, 12,* 129–132.

Weiss, B., & Weisz, J. R. (1995). Relative effectiveness of behavioral versus nonbehavioral child psychotherapy. *Journal of Consulting and Clinical Psychology,
63,* 317–320.

Weisz, J. R., Jensen-Doss, A., & Hawley, K. M. (2006). Evidence-based youth psychotherapies versus clinical care: A meta-analysis of direct comparisons. *American Psychologist, 61,* 671–689.

Weisz, J. R., McCarty, C. A., & Valeri, S. M. (2006). Effects of psychotherapy for depression in children and adolescents: A meta-analysis. *Psychological Bulletin, 132,* 132–149.

Weisz, J. R., Weiss, B., Han, S. S., Granger, D. A., & Morton, T. (1995). Effects of psychotherapy with children and adolescents revisited: A meta-analysis of treatment outcome studies. *Psychological Bulletin, 117,* 450–468.

Westen, D. (1998). The scientific legacy of Sigmund Freud: Toward a psycho-dynamically informed psychological science. *Psychological Bulletin, 124,* 333–371.

Westen, D., & Morrison, K. (2001). A multidimensional meta-analysis of treatments for depression, panic, and generalized anxiety disorders: An examination of the status of empirically supported therapies. *Journal of Consulting and Clinical Psychology, 69,* 875–899.

Westen, D., Novotny, C. M., & Thompson-Brenner, H. (2004). The empirical status of empirically supported psychotherapies: Assumptions, findings, and reporting in controlled clinical trials. *Psychological Bulletin, 130,* 631–663.

Whipple, J. L., Lambert, M. J., Vermeersch, D. A., Smart, D. W., Nielsen, S. L., & Hawkins, E. J. (2003). Improving the effects of psychotherapy: The use of early identification of treatment failure and problem solving strategies in routine practice. *Journal of Counseling Psychology, 58,* 59–68.

Whittal, M. L., Thordarson, D. S., & McLean, P. D. (2005). Treatment of obsessive-compulsive disorder: Cognitive behavior therapy vs. exposure and response prevention. *Behaviour Research and Therapy, 43,* 1559–1576.

Widiger, T. A., & Trull, T. J. (2007). Plate tectonics in the classification of personality disorders: Shifting to a dimensional model. *American Psychologist, 62,* 71–83.

Williams, D. R., Neighbors, H. W., & Jackson, J. S. (2008). Racial/ethnic discrimination and health: Findings from community studies. *American Journal of Public Health, 98,* S29–S37.

Wilson, G. T. (1982). How useful is meta-analysis in evaluating the effects of different psychological therapies? *Behavioural Psychotherapy, 10,* 221–231.

Wilson, G. T., & Rachman, S. J. (1983). Meta-analysis and the evaluation of psychotherapy outcome: Limitations and liabilities. *Journal of Consulting and Clinical Psychology, 51,* 54–64.

Wolpe, J. (1958). *Psychotherapy by reciprocal inhibition.* Palo Alto, CA: Stanford University.

Wrenn, C. G. (1962). *Counselor in a changing world.* Washington, DC: American Personnel and Guidance Association.

Yalom, I. D. (1995). *The theory and practice of group psychotherapy* (4th ed.). New York, NY: Basic Books.

Zane, N., Sue, S., Young, K., Nunez, J., & Hall, G. N. (2004). Research on psychotherapy with culturally diverse populations. In M. J. Lambert (Ed.), *Bergin and Garfield's handbook of psychotherapy and behavior change* (5th ed., pp. 767–804). New York, NY: Wiley.

Zuroff, D. C., & Blatt, S. J. (2006). The therapeutic relationship in brief treatment of depression: Contributions to clinical improvement and enhanced adaptive capacities. *Journal of Consulting and Clinical Psychology, 74,* 130–140.

Index

Object relations school, 24–25
Observation
  as foundation of science, 21
  in positivism, 56
Obsessive-compulsive disorder, 76, 92
Ollendick, T. H., 71

Panic disorder
  etiology of, 91
  studies on treatment of, 75–76, 79
Pasek, L. F., 78
Pasteur, Louis, 57
Paul, G. L., 34
Pavlov, Ivan Petrovich, 21
Pedersen, P., 40
Peptic ulcers, 86, 91
Perls, Frederick "Fritz," 24
Personality and Psychotherapy
  (J. Dollard and N. E. Miller), 32
Personality disorder treatment, 77
Person-centered therapy, 23–24
Persuasion and Healing (Jerome Frank), 36
Pharmacotherapy, 101. *See also* Medication
Phenomenology, 46, 57–58, 107
Philosophy of science, 55–59
Placebo control groups, 85–86, 88–91
Positivism
  components of therapies based in, 46
  history of, 55–56
  and observation, 21
Postmodernism, 39–42, 46, 58, 107–108
Posttraumatic stress disorder (PTSD)
  cognitve processing therapy for
    treatment of, 87
  studies on treatment of, 74–75
Procedures, 36
Process experiential therapy, 24
Prochaska, J. O., 103
Progressive relaxation, 21
Protocols, treatment, 11
Psychic treatments, 18–19
Psychoanalysis, 17

Psychoanalysis and Behavior Therapy (P. L. Wachtel), 33
Psychoanalytic psychotherapy, 75
Psychodynamic therapies
  components of, 46
  defined, 24
  procedures in, 36
  for treatment of personality disorders, 77
Psychological placebos, 69
Psychopathology, 44
Psychopharmacological treatments, 97.
  See also Medication
Psychotherapy. *See also specific headings*
  definitions of, 8–12
  as healing practice, 5–9
Psychotherapy by Reciprocal Inhibition
  (Joseph Wolpe), 21
Psychotherapy theory(-ies), 15–60
  and clients, 51–55
  and common factors, 35–39, 43
  competing theories, 20–26
  elements of, 43–46
  legitimate vs. illegitimate, 26
  and philosophy of science, 55–59
  postmodern developments in, 39–42
  as road maps for therapists, 108
  social context for origins of, 16–20
  Society of Clinical Psychology criteria
    for, 27–31
  technical eclecticism approach to, 34
  theoretical integration approach to,
    32–34
  and therapists, 45, 47–51
PTSD. *See* Posttraumatic stress disorder
"Purity of treatment," 54

Quantum theory, 57

Randomized control groups, 61–62
Rationale, 36
Rational emotive therapy, 67
Rayner, Rosalie, 21, 22

Realism, 56–57
Relapse rates, 94
Remoralization, 109
Researcher allegiance, 72–73
Resick, P. A., 87
Response prevention/exposure, 92
Rituals, 36
Rogers, Carl, 24
Rosenthal, D., 88
Rosenzweig, S., 35–36, 70

Santayana, George, 12
Schneider, Kirk, 24
Science
    in history of psychotherapy, 16
    philosophy of, 55–59
Scientific Advisory Board, 31
Sechrest, L., 94
Self-efficacy, 109
Shapiro, D., 68–70
Shapiro, D. A., 68–70
Siev, J., 79
Singer, M. T., 27
Skill building, 103
Skills, with cultural interaction, 40–41
Smith, B., 94
Smith, M. L., 63–64, 67, 68
Social anxieties, 76
Social constructivism, 58
Social constructs, 41
Social relations, 45
Society of Clinical Psychology, 27–31
Specific effects, 19, 85–95
    component designs, 86–91
    establishing system-specific sequence,
        91–95
Spielmans, G. I., 78
Standard care, 80
Stevens, S. E., 90
Stigma, of psychotherapy, 7
Stiles, W. B., 82
Substance use disorder treatment, 76
Sudden gains, 93
Sullivan, Henry Stack, 25

Supportive counseling, 69, 88
Symptom change, 103
Systematic desensitization
    effectiveness of, 67
    history of, 21
Systematic eclectic psychotherapy, 34
System-specific sequence, 91–95

Talebi, H., 103
Talk therapy, 9, 16–17, 107
Tang, T. Z., 93
Task Force on Promotion and
    Dissemination of Psychology
    Procedures (Society of Clinical
    Psychology), 27–31
Tasks, of therapy, 97
TAU (treatment as usual), 80–81
TDCRP. *See* Treatment of Depression
    Collaborative Research Program
Technical eclecticism approach, 34
Telephone counseling, 9
Theoretical integration approach
    to psychotherapy theories, 32–34
    for theory selection, 50
Theory, in positivism, 55. *See also*
    Psychotherapy theory(-ies)
Therapists
    and common factors, 99–102
    and psychotherapy theories, 45, 47–51
Tomcho, T. J., 48
Transference, 25
Treatment as usual (TAU), 80–81
Treatment conditions, 37
Treatment of Depression Collaborative
    Research Program (TDCRP),
    92–93, 100–101
Treatment planning, 47
Treatment protocols, 11
Truthiness, of theories, 49–50, 110

UKATT Research Team, 94–95
United States, 39
U.S. Food and Drug Administration, 62
Usual care, 80

About the Author

Bruce E. Wampold received his PhD from the counseling psychology program at the University of California, Santa Barbara, in 1981 and joined the University of Wisconsin Madison faculty in 1991. He has been a faculty member in the counseling psychology programs at the University of California, Santa Barbara; the University of Utah; and the University of Oregon. Prior to his doctoral studies, he was a junior and senior high school mathematics teacher, counselor, and coach.

Currently, Dr. Wampold's area of interest is in the efficacy of counseling and psychotherapy. He has published various meta-analyses and analyses of data from naturalistic settings that have demonstrated that the efficacy of psychotherapy emanates from the contextual features and not the specific ingredients. This work culminated in the book *The Great Psychotherapy Debate: Models, Methods, and Findings* (2001). Recently, he has conceptualized psychotherapy as a healing practice embedded in historical and cultural contexts. His work has influenced the practice of psychotherapy through consultations with managed care companies and health care accrediting organizations as well as presentations to scientists and practitioners around the world. He served on the American Psychological Association (APA) Presidential Task Force on Evidence-Based Practice in Psychology and the Performance Improvement Advisory Group. His research on these topics has been published in *Psychological Bulletin, Journal of Consulting and Clinical Psychology, Journal of Counseling*

Psychology, Journal of Clinical Psychology, and *Journal of Affective Disorders,* among others.

Another area of interest centers on social interactions. Dr. Wampold has developed methods to analyze discourse and has applied these methods to understand marriage, counseling, supervision, family, work, classroom interactions, and scientific laboratories. Dr. Wampold has developed research and statistical methods that have applications in many areas of psychology and education. Also, he has published several articles, book chapters, and books describing research methods for educators, counselors, and applied psychologists, including *Theory and Application of Statistics* (with C. J. Drew, 1989) and *Research Design in Counseling* (with P. P. Heppner and D. M. Kivlighan, 2005).

Dr. Wampold is a licensed psychologist and a diplomate in counseling psychology of the American Board of Professional Psychology. He is the 2007 recipient of the APA Award for Distinguished Professional Contributions to Applied Research; the 2008 Lifetime Achievement Award, Section on the Promotion of Psychotherapy Science, Society of Counseling Psychology (Division 17 of APA); and the 2008 Distinguished Psychologist Award, Division 29 (Psychotherapy). He is an APA fellow of Divisions 12 (Society of Clinical Psychology), 17 (Society of Counseling Psychology), 29 (Psychotherapy), and 45 (Society for the Psychological Study of Ethnic Minority Issues); was vice president of the Society of Counseling Psychology for Scientific Affairs; and is past associate editor of the *Journal of Counseling Psychology* and of *Behavioral Assessment.*

Cogent - convincing or believable by
virtue of clear presentation
relevant; pertinent

efficacy - capacity for producing a
desired result
effectiveness